I0426310

January 2012

TROUBLED ASSET RELIEF PROGRAM

As Treasury Continues to Exit Programs, Opportunities to Enhance Communication on Costs Exist

GAO

Accountability ★ Integrity ★ Reliability

GAO-12-229

TROUBLED ASSET RELIEF PROGRAM

As Treasury Continues to Exit Programs, Opportunities to Enhance Communication on Costs Exist

Highlights of GAO-12-229, a report to congressional addressees

Why GAO Did This Study

The Emergency Economic Stabilization Act of 2008 authorized the Department of the Treasury (Treasury) to create the Troubled Asset Relief Program (TARP), a $700 billion program designed to restore the liquidity and stability of the financial system. The act also requires that GAO report every 60 days on TARP activities. This report examines (1) the condition and status of TARP programs; (2) Treasury's management of TARP operations, including staffing for the Office of Financial Stability (OFS) and oversight of contractors and financial agents; and (3) what is known about the direct and indirect costs of TARP. To do this work, GAO analyzed audited financial data for various TARP programs; reviewed documentation such as program terms and internal decision memos; analyzed TARP cost estimates from the Congressional Budget Office (CBO), the Office of Management and Budget, and Treasury; and interviewed CBO and OFS officials.

What GAO Recommends

Treasury should enhance its program-specific press releases to the public by consistently including lifetime cost estimates when reporting on program activities and results. Treasury agreed with our recommendation and plans to implement it by including a link to its cost reporting in future TARP program-specific press releases.

View GAO-12-229 or key components.
For more information, contact Thomas J. McCool at (202) 512-2642 or mccoolt@gao.gov.

What GAO Found

Many TARP programs continue to be in various stages of unwinding and some programs, notably those that focus on the foreclosure crisis, remain active. The figure provides an overview of selected programs and the amount disbursed and outstanding, as applicable. Treasury has articulated broad principles for exiting TARP, including exiting TARP programs as soon as practicable and seeking to maximize taxpayer returns, goals that at times conflict. Some of the programs that Treasury continues to unwind, such as investments in American International Group, Inc. (AIG), require Treasury to actively manage the timing of its exit as it balances its competing goals. For other programs, such as the Capital Purchase Program (CPP)—which was created to provide capital to financial institutions—Treasury's exit will be driven primarily by the financial condition of the participating institutions. Consequently, the timing of Treasury's exit from TARP remains uncertain.

Treasury continues to manage the various TARP programs using OFS staff, financial agents, and contractors. Overall OFS staffing has declined slightly for the first time as staff responsible for managing TARP investment programs and those in term-appointed leadership positions have departed. However, staff in some offices within OFS have increased—for example, in the Office of Internal Review, which helps to ensure that financial agents and contractors comply with laws and regulations. Through September 30, 2011, about half of Treasury's 116 contracts remained active, along with 14 of the 17 financial agency agreements. Treasury has continued to strengthen its management and oversight of contractors and financial agents and conflict-of-interest requirements. In response to a GAO recommendation, OFS has finalized a plan to address staffing levels and expertise that includes identifying critical positions and conducting succession planning, in light of the temporary nature of its work.

Treasury and CBO project that TARP costs will be much lower than the amount authorized when the program was initially announced. Treasury's fiscal year 2011 financial statement, audited by GAO, estimated that the lifetime cost of TARP would be about $70 billion—with CPP expected to generate the most lifetime income, or net income in excess of costs. OFS also reported that from inception through September 30, 2011, the incurred cost of TARP transactions was $28 billion. Although Treasury regularly reports on the cost of TARP programs and has enhanced such reporting over time, GAO's analysis of Treasury press releases about specific programs indicate that information about estimated lifetime costs and income are included only when programs are expected to result in lifetime income. For example, Treasury issued a press release for its bank investment programs, including CPP, and noted that the programs would result in lifetime income, or profit. However, press releases for investments in AIG, a program that is anticipated to result in a lifetime cost to Treasury, did not include program-specific cost information. Although press releases for programs expected to result in a cost to Treasury provide useful transaction information, they exclude lifetime, program-specific cost estimates.

Consistently providing greater transparency about cost information for specific TARP programs could help reduce potential misunderstanding of TARP's results. While Treasury can measure and report direct costs, indirect costs associated with the moral hazard created by the government's intervention in the private sector are more difficult to measure and assess.

Status of Selected Programs, as of September 30, 2011

	Program	Amounts (dollars in billions)
Closed programs with outstanding assets	**Capital Purchase Program** To provide capital to viable banks through the purchase of preferred shares and subordinated debentures.	$17.3 outstanding assets — Disbursed: $204.9
	Automotive Industry Financing Program To prevent a significant disruption of the American automotive industry.	$37.3 outstanding assets — Disbursed: $79.7
	AIG Investment Program To provide stability in financial markets and avoid disruptions to the markets from the deterioration of AIG's financial condition.	$51.1 outstanding assets — Disbursed: $67.8
Active programs	**TARP-funded housing programs** To offer assistance to homeowners at risk of foreclosure.[a]	$2.4 in payments — Authorized: $45.6
	Public-Private Investment Program To address the challenge of "legacy assets" by partnering with investors to purchase certain residential and commercial mortgage-backed securities.	$15.9 outstanding assets — Disbursed: $17.6

	Program	Lifetime income (dollars in billions)
Programs Treasury exited	**Asset Guarantee Program** To provide federal government assurances for assets held by financial institutions that were viewed as critical to the functioning of the nation's financial system.[b]	$3.7
	Targeted Investment Program To foster market stability and strengthen the economy by making case-by-case investments in institutions that Treasury deemed critical to the functioning of the financial system.	$4
	Capital Assessment Program Created to provide capital to institutions not able to raise it privately to meet Supervisory Capital Assessment Program—or "stress test"—requirements. This program was never used.	n/a

Source: GAO analysis of Treasury data.

Note: TARP programs with disbursements of less than $600 million are excluded. Outstanding assets are presented at book value.

[a]TARP-funded housing programs include a variety of programs to assist homeowners. Unlke the investment programs, TARP-funded housing programs do not hold assets to manage and sell; therefore, there are no outstanding assets.

[b]Treasury no longer holds assets for this program that it must manage, though the Federal Deposit Insurance Corporation still holds Citigroup trust preferred stock and Treasury could receive income when these assets are sold.

Contents

Figures

Abbreviations

ABS	asset-backed securities
AIFP	Automotive Industry Financing Program
AIG	American International Group, Inc.
CBO	Congressional Budget Office
CDCI	Community Development Capital Initiative
CDFI	Community Development Financial Institutions
CMBS	commercial mortgage-backed securities
CPP	Capital Purchase Program
Dodd-Frank Act	Dodd-Frank Wall Street Reform and Consumer Protection Act
EESA	Emergency Economic Stabilization Act
Federal Reserve	Board of Governors of the Federal Reserve System
FRBNY	Federal Reserve Bank of New York
FHA	Federal Housing Administration
GM	General Motors
HAMP	Home Affordable Modification Program
IPO	initial public offering
IRS	Internal Revenue Service
MHA	Making Home Affordable
Moody's	Moody's Investors Service, Inc.
OFS	Office of Financial Stability
OIR	Office of Internal Review
OMB	Office of Management and Budget
PPIF	public-private investment fund
PPIP	Public-Private Investment Program
SBA	Small Business Administration
SPV	special purpose vehicle
TALF	Term Asset-backed Securities Loan Facility
TARP	Troubled Asset Relief Program
Treasury	Department of the Treasury

January 9, 2012

Congressional Addressees

The Emergency Economic Stabilization Act (EESA) initially authorized $700 billion to assist financial institutions and markets, businesses, homeowners, and consumers through the Troubled Asset Relief Program (TARP).[1] This amount was intended to provide confidence that the U.S. government would help address the greatest threat the financial markets and economy had faced since the Great Depression. As the severity and immediacy of the 2008 financial crisis began to diminish, Congress reduced the authorized amount to $475 billion with the Dodd-Frank Wall Street Reform and Consumer Protection Act (Dodd-Frank Act).[2] TARP cost estimates were never projected to reach the authorized amounts and over time these projected costs have declined as some banks have repaid their assistance and other programs move closer to their termination dates.[3] However, an increasing number of banks that received Capital Purchase Program investments are falling behind on paying dividends related to their government assistance, and TARP-funded housing programs continue to struggle to address the ongoing foreclosure crisis.

The Department of the Treasury (Treasury) is the primary agency implementing TARP and its activities have been broad in scope. Treasury established the Office of Financial Stability (OFS) to carry out TARP activities, which include injecting capital into key financial institutions,

---

[1]EESA, Pub. L. No. 110-343, 122 Stat. 3765 (2008) (codified at 12 U.S.C. §§ 5201 et seq.). EESA originally authorized Treasury to purchase or guarantee up to $700 billion in troubled assets. The Helping Families Save Their Homes Act of 2009, Pub. L. No. 111-22, Div. A, 123 Stat. 1632 (2009), amended EESA to reduce the maximum allowable amount of outstanding troubled assets under EESA by almost $1.3 billion, from $700 billion to $698.741 billion.

[2]The Dodd-Frank Act, Pub. L. No. 111-203, 124 Stat. 1376 (2010), (1) reduced Treasury's authority to purchase or insure troubled assets to a maximum of $475 billion and (2) prohibited Treasury, under EESA, from incurring any additional obligations for a program or initiative unless the program or initiative had already been initiated prior to June 25, 2010.

[3]The Department of the Treasury, the Congressional Budget Office, and the Office of Management and Budget provided cost estimates that were all below $700 billion; the highest estimate was about half of the $700 billion allocated for TARP.

implementing programs to address problems in the securitization markets, providing assistance to the automobile industry, and offering incentives for modifying residential mortgages, among other activities.

As required by EESA, we have provided oversight of TARP activities since they began in 2008. This 60-day report assesses the condition of TARP as of September 30, 2011.[4] Specifically, it examines (1) the condition and status of TARP programs; (2) Treasury's management of TARP operations, including staffing for OFS and oversight of contractors and financial agents; and (3) what is known about the direct and indirect costs of TARP.

To assess the condition and status of TARP programs, we analyzed program-specific data on obligations, disbursements, income, and other financial information from our audits of OFS's financial statements; reviewed program documentation such as program terms and internal decision memos; and interviewed OFS officials responsible for TARP programs and financial reporting.[5] We determined that the financial information used in this report is sufficiently reliable to assess the condition and status of TARP programs. We also leveraged our past reporting on TARP, as well as that of the Congressional Oversight Panel and the Special Inspector General for TARP, as appropriate.[6] To understand OFS's progress in staffing and its oversight of contractors and financial agents we collected staffing data and trends from 2008 through September 30, 2011; analyzed select contracts and financial agreements; and interviewed OFS officials. We determined that the staffing data were sufficiently reliable for our purposes by corroborating the data with other sources. To determine what information was available about the costs of

---

[4]We have issued a TARP report at least every 60 days as required by EESA in Section 116, 12 U.S.C. § 5226 (codified at 12 U.S.C. § 5226). Unless otherwise noted, we provide information throughout this report as of September 30, 2011.

[5]See GAO, *Financial Audit: Office of Financial Stability (Troubled Asset Relief Program) Fiscal Years 2011 and 2010 Financial Statements,* GAO-12-169 (Washington, D.C.: Nov.10, 2011), *Financial Audit: Office of Financial Stability (Troubled Asset Relief Program) Fiscal Years 2010 and 2009 Financial Statements,* GAO-11-174 (Washington, D.C.: Nov.15, 2010), and *Financial Audit: Office of Financial Stability (Troubled Asset Relief Program) Fiscal Year 2009 Financial Statements,* GAO-10-301 (Washington, D.C.: Dec. 9, 2009).

[6]Pursuant to EESA's requirements, the Congressional Oversight Panel terminated on April 3, 2011.

TARP, we analyzed cost data from reports issued by the Congressional Budget Office (CBO), the Office of Management and Budget (OMB), and Treasury, focusing on Treasury cost estimates for our analyses. We also interviewed officials from CBO and Treasury about cost estimate methodologies.

We conducted this performance audit from June 2011 to January 2012 in accordance with generally accepted government auditing standards. Those standards require that we plan and perform the audit to obtain sufficient, appropriate evidence to provide a reasonable basis for our findings and conclusions based on our audit objectives. We believe that the evidence obtained provides a reasonable basis for our findings and conclusions based on our audit objectives.

Background

When EESA was signed on October 3, 2008, the U.S. financial system faced a severe crisis that has rippled throughout the global economy, moving from the U.S. housing market to an array of financial assets and interbank lending. The crisis restricted access to credit and made the financing on which businesses and individuals depend increasingly difficult to obtain. Further tightening of credit exacerbated a global economic slowdown. During the crisis, Congress, the President, federal regulators, and others undertook a number of steps to facilitate financial intermediation by banks and the securities markets. In addition to Treasury's efforts, policy interventions were led by the Board of Governors of the Federal Reserve System (Federal Reserve) and the Federal Deposit Insurance Corporation. While the banking crisis in the United States no longer presents the same level of systemic concerns as it did in 2008, the economy remains vulnerable, with unemployment higher than in the recent past. Globally, concerns about the stability of European banks and countries, especially Greece, escalated in 2011— demonstrating that problems remain in the global economy and financial markets.

TARP Programs and Implementation

The passage of EESA resulted in a variety of programs supported with TARP funding.[7] (See table 1.)

Table 1: List of Programs Supported by TARP Funding

Program	Program description
American International Group, Inc. (AIG) Investment Program (formerly Systemically Significant Failing Institutions Program)	Provided support to AIG to avoid disruptions to financial markets as its financial condition deteriorated.
Asset Guarantee Program	Provided federal government assurances for assets held by financial institutions that were viewed as critical to the functioning of the nation's financial system. Bank of America and Citigroup were the only two institutions that participated in this program.
Automotive Industry Financing Program (AIFP)	Aimed to prevent a significant disruption of the American automotive industry through government investments in certain domestic automakers—Chrysler and General Motors (GM)—and auto financing companies Ally Financial (formerly known as General Motors Acceptance Corporation, or GMAC) and Chrysler Financial.
Capital Assessment Program	Created to provide capital to institutions not able to raise it privately to meet Supervisory Capital Assessment Program—or "stress test"—requirements. This program was never used.
Capital Purchase Program (CPP)	As the largest TARP program, CPP was designed to provide capital investments to financially viable financial institutions. Treasury received preferred shares and subordinated debentures, along with warrants.[a]
Consumer and Business Lending Initiative programs	• *Community Development Capital Initiative (CDCI)* provided capital to Community Development Financial Institutions (CDFI) by purchasing preferred stock and subordinated debentures. • *Small Business Administration (SBA) 7(a) Securities Purchase Program* provided liquidity to secondary markets for government-guaranteed small business loans in SBA's 7(a) loan program. • *Term Asset-backed Securities Loan Facility (TALF)* provided liquidity in securitization markets for various asset classes to improve access to credit for consumers and businesses.

---

[7]For more information on these programs, see our two previous reports on TARP after its first and second year of implementation: GAO, *Troubled Asset Relief Program: Status of Programs and Implementation of GAO Recommendations,* GAO-11-74 (Washington, D.C.: Jan. 12, 2011), and *Troubled Asset Relief Program: One Year Later, Actions Are Needed to Address Remaining Transparency and Accountability Challenges,* GAO-10-16 (Washington, D.C.: Oct. 8, 2009).

GAO-12-229 Troubled Asset Relief Program

Program	Program description
TARP-funded housing programs	• *Making Home Affordable includes several housing programs.* The primary program has been the Home Affordable Modification Program (HAMP), under which Treasury shares the cost of reducing monthly payments on first lien mortgages with mortgage holders/investors and provides financial incentives to servicers, borrowers, and mortgage holders/investors for loans modified under the program.[c] • *Hardest Hit Fund* seeks to help homeowners in the states hit hardest by unemployment and house price declines. • *Support for the Department of Housing and Urban Development's Federal Housing Administration (FHA) Short Refinance program* enables homeowners whose mortgages exceed the value of their homes to refinance into more affordable mortgages.
Public-Private Investment Program (PPIP)	Created to address the challenge of "legacy assets" as part of Treasury's efforts to repair balance sheets throughout the financial system. Treasury partnered with private funds to purchase residential and commercial mortgage-backed securities.
Targeted Investment Program (TIP)	Sought to foster market stability and strengthen the economy by making case-by-case investments in institutions that Treasury deemed critical to the functioning of the financial system. Bank of America and Citigroup were the only two institutions that participated in this program.

Source: GAO.

[a]A warrant is an option to buy shares of common stock or preferred stock at a predetermined price on or before a specified date.

[b]CDFIs are financial institutions that provide financing and related services to communities and populations that lack access to credit, capital, and financial services.

[c]For more information on additional Making Home Affordable programs funded through TARP see GAO, *Troubled Asset Relief Program: Treasury Continues to Face Implementation Challenges and Data Weaknesses in Its Making Home Affordable Program*, GAO-11-288 (Washington, D.C.: Mar. 17, 2011).

Some of these programs have begun to unwind.[8] Figure 1 provides an overview of key dates for TARP implementation and the unwinding of some programs.

---

[8]In addition to programs that are moving towards exit, the Asset Guarantee Program, the Capital Assessment Program, and the Targeted Investment Program are no longer active and Treasury no longer holds assets related to these programs that it must manage, as we have previously reported. For more information, see appendix II.

Figure 1: Timeline for TARP Implementation and Unwinding, October 3, 2008, through December 31, 2011

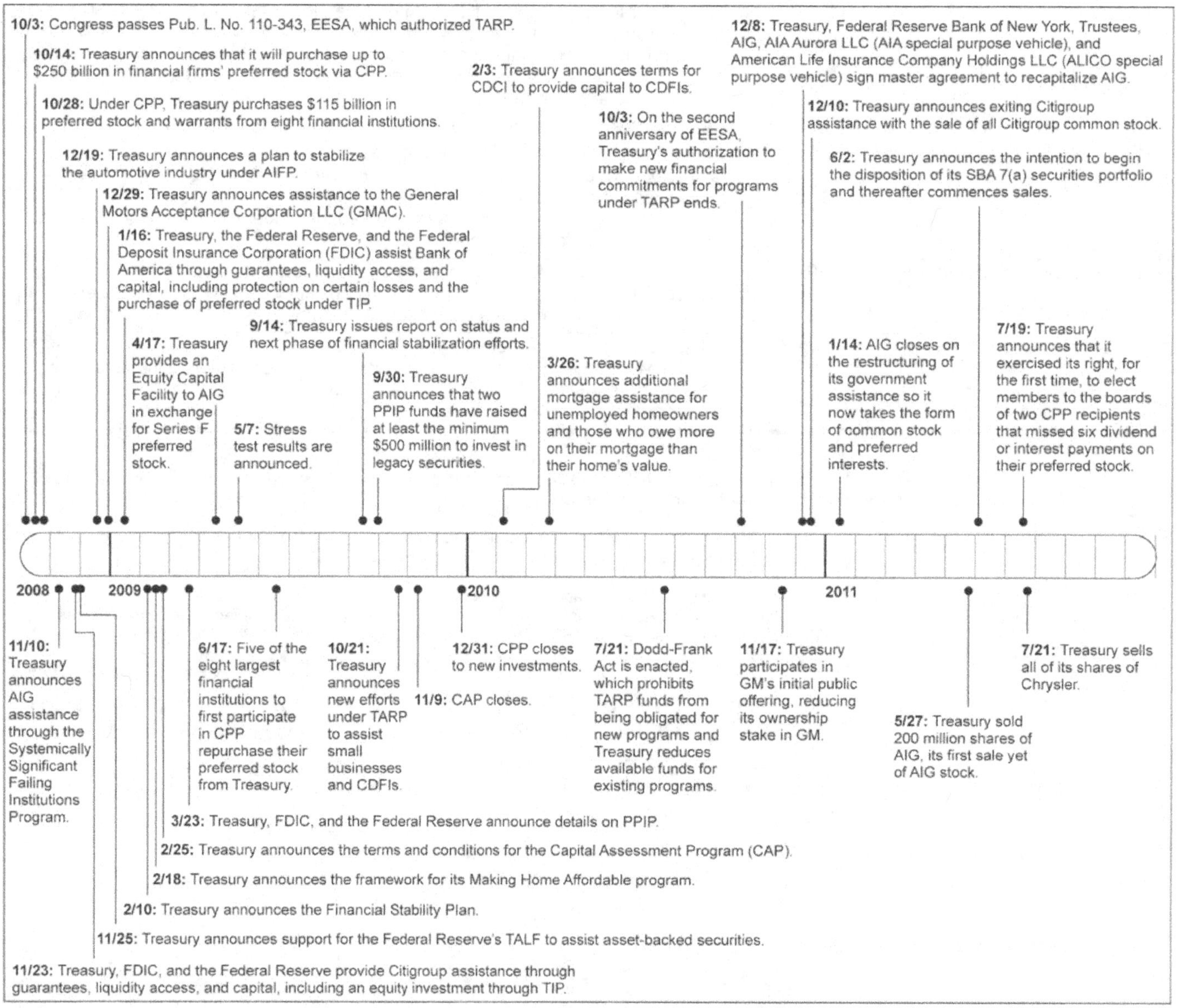

10/3: Congress passes Pub. L. No. 110-343, EESA, which authorized TARP.

10/14: Treasury announces that it will purchase up to $250 billion in financial firms' preferred stock via CPP.

10/28: Under CPP, Treasury purchases $115 billion in preferred stock and warrants from eight financial institutions.

12/19: Treasury announces a plan to stabilize the automotive industry under AIFP.

12/29: Treasury announces assistance to the General Motors Acceptance Corporation LLC (GMAC).

1/16: Treasury, the Federal Reserve, and the Federal Deposit Insurance Corporation (FDIC) assist Bank of America through guarantees, liquidity access, and capital, including protection on certain losses and the purchase of preferred stock under TIP.

4/17: Treasury provides an Equity Capital Facility to AIG in exchange for Series F preferred stock.

5/7: Stress test results are announced.

9/14: Treasury issues report on status and next phase of financial stabilization efforts.

9/30: Treasury announces that two PPIP funds have raised at least the minimum $500 million to invest in legacy securities.

2/3: Treasury announces terms for CDCI to provide capital to CDFIs.

10/3: On the second anniversary of EESA, Treasury's authorization to make new financial commitments for programs under TARP ends.

3/26: Treasury announces additional mortgage assistance for unemployed homeowners and those who owe more on their mortgage than their home's value.

12/8: Treasury, Federal Reserve Bank of New York, Trustees, AIG, AIA Aurora LLC (AIA special purpose vehicle), and American Life Insurance Company Holdings LLC (ALICO special purpose vehicle) sign master agreement to recapitalize AIG.

12/10: Treasury announces exiting Citigroup assistance with the sale of all Citigroup common stock.

6/2: Treasury announces the intention to begin the disposition of its SBA 7(a) securities portfolio and thereafter commences sales.

1/14: AIG closes on the restructuring of its government assistance so it now takes the form of common stock and preferred interests.

7/19: Treasury announces that it exercised its right, for the first time, to elect members to the boards of two CPP recipients that missed six dividend or interest payments on their preferred stock.

2008   2009   2010   2011

11/10: Treasury announces AIG assistance through the Systemically Significant Failing Institutions Program.

6/17: Five of the eight largest financial institutions to first participate in CPP repurchase their preferred stock from Treasury.

10/21: Treasury announces new efforts under TARP to assist small businesses and CDFIs.

11/9: CAP closes.

12/31: CPP closes to new investments.

7/21: Dodd-Frank Act is enacted, which prohibits TARP funds from being obligated for new programs and Treasury reduces available funds for existing programs.

11/17: Treasury participates in GM's initial public offering, reducing its ownership stake in GM.

5/27: Treasury sold 200 million shares of AIG, its first sale yet of AIG stock.

7/21: Treasury sells all of its shares of Chrysler.

3/23: Treasury, FDIC, and the Federal Reserve announce details on PPIP.

2/25: Treasury announces the terms and conditions for the Capital Assessment Program (CAP).

2/18: Treasury announces the framework for its Making Home Affordable program.

2/10: Treasury announces the Financial Stability Plan.

11/25: Treasury announces support for the Federal Reserve's TALF to assist asset-backed securities.

11/23: Treasury, FDIC, and the Federal Reserve provide Citigroup assistance through guarantees, liquidity access, and capital, including an equity investment through TIP.

Source: GAO analysis of Treasury data.

TARP Cost Estimates

EESA requires that Treasury, OMB, and CBO report the costs of TARP. Section 105 of EESA directed Treasury to provide Congress with regular cost and transaction updates for TARP and section 202 addresses OMB's and CBO's reporting duties. Specifically, OMB must prepare semiannual reports for the President and Congress that include lifetime cost estimates for Treasury's TARP-related purchases and guarantees.[9] Treasury provides OMB with the program-specific transaction data and cost calculations, which OMB reviews and approves before incorporating into its semiannual reports. Section 202 also directed CBO to conduct assessments of each OMB report, including the cost of purchases and guarantees. These analyses must be included in a separate CBO report issued within 45 days of each OMB semiannual report.[10]

Treasury, OMB, and CBO report lifetime subsidy cost estimates (cost estimates) for TARP and its direct loan, equity investment, and other credit programs using the credit reform budgetary accounting methodology established in the Federal Credit Reform Act of 1990.[11] Credit reform accounting requires that agencies develop a "subsidy" cost of loans and loan guarantees at disbursement that considers projections of future cash flows and the costs of financing. Administrative costs such as personnel and travel expenses are not included. The subsidy cost is the net present value of all cash flows associated with the transaction calculated by discounting all future payments back to the current period at one of two specific rates. The Federal Credit Reform Act of 1990 calls for the use of an interest rate on comparable Treasury debt while EESA requires Treasury to use an interest rate adjusted for market risk. These subsidy costs are re-estimated annually to include actual cash flows and changes in estimated future performance. According to Treasury, its lifetime cost estimates represent the department's best estimate of what TARP and its programs will ultimately cost the taxpayer.[12]

---

[9]Section 123 of EESA requires the use of credit reform accounting established by the Federal Credit Reform Act of 1990 to calculate cost estimates for budgetary purposes for TARP transactions that include equity investments, loans, and loan guarantees.

[10]See Sections 105 and 202 of EESA.

[11]Other credit programs consist of the Asset Guarantee Program and the FHA Short Refinance Program. Federal Credit Reform Act of 1990, Pub. L. No. 101-508, Title XII, Subtitle B, § 13201, 104 Stat. 1388, 1388-61 (1990).

[12]In some cases, these cost estimates suggest certain TARP programs could result in net income for the taxpayer because the proceeds from Treasury's investments (e.g., repayments, dividends, and interest payments) are expected to exceed costs. We refer to these estimates as "lifetime income" estimates throughout the report.

While Many TARP Programs Continue to Wind Down, Others Remain Active

TARP programs continue to wind down, and some programs have ended. Treasury has stated its goals for the exit process for many programs, but as we and others have reported, these goals at times conflict.[13] Treasury has stated that when deciding to sell assets and exit TARP programs, it will strive to:

- protect taxpayer investment and maximize overall investment returns within competing constraints,

- promote the stability of financial markets and the economy by preventing disruptions,

- bolster markets' confidence to increase private capital investment, and

- dispose of the investments as soon as it is practicable.

For example, we previously reported that deciding to unwind some of its assistance to GM by participating in an initial public offering (IPO) presented Treasury with a conflict between maximizing taxpayer returns and exiting as soon as practicable. Holding its shares longer could have meant realizing greater gains for the taxpayer, but only if the stock appreciated in value. By participating in GM's November 2010 IPO, Treasury tried to fulfill both goals, selling almost half of its shares at an early opportunity. Treasury officials stated that they strove to balance these competing goals, but have no strict formula for doing so. Rather, they ultimately relied on the best available information in deciding when to start exiting this program.

Moreover, Treasury's ability to exercise control over the timing of its exit from TARP programs is limited in some cases. For example, Treasury will likely decide when to exit AIG based on market conditions but Treasury has less control over its exit from PPIP because the program's exit depends on the timing of each public-private investment fund (PPIF) selling its investments. Treasury continues to face this tension in its goals

---

[13]See GAO, *TARP: Treasury's Exit from GM and Chrysler Highlights Competing Goals, and Results of Support to Auto Communities Are Unclear*, GAO-11-471 (Washington, D.C.: May 10, 2011). The Congressional Oversight Panel also noted these competing goals. See Congressional Oversight Panel, *January Oversight Report: Exiting TARP and Unwinding Its Impact on the Financial Markets* (Washington, D.C.: Jan. 14, 2010).

with a number of TARP programs as they continue to unwind. Throughout this section we provide the status of each TARP program that remains open or still holds assets that need to be managed, including when the program will end (or stop acquiring new assets and no longer receive funding) and when Treasury will exit the program (or sell assets it acquired while the program was open). We also provide information on outstanding assets, as applicable—both the book value and the market value—as of September 30, 2011.[14] Also included are the lifetime estimated costs for each program calculated by Treasury. Later in this report we discuss the reasons for recent changes in several of Treasury's cost estimates between September 2010 and September 2011.

Many Programs Continue to Wind Down, and Treasury Faces Trade-offs in Determining When to Exit

Financial Strength Will Determine When Remaining CPP Institutions Exit Program

While repayments and income from CPP investments have exceeded the original outlays, financial strength will determine when remaining institutions exit the program. As we have reported, Treasury disbursed $204.9 billion to 707 financial institutions nationwide from October 2008 through December 2009.[15] As of September 30, 2011, Treasury had received $208.1 billion in repayment and income from its CPP investments, exceeding the amount originally disbursed by $3.2 billion (see fig. 2). The repayment and income amount included $182.4 billion in repayments of original CPP investments, as well as $11.2 billion in dividends, interest, and fees; $7.6 billion in warrant income; and $6.9 billion in net proceeds in excess of costs. After accounting for writeoffs and realized losses on sales totaling $2.6 billion, CPP had $17.3 billion in

---

[14]Note that some numbers in our program figures will not total due to rounding.

[15]GAO-11-74. We also reported on CPP in *Troubled Asset Relief Program: Opportunities Exist to Apply Lessons Learned from the Capital Purchase Program to Similarly Designed Programs and to Improve the Repayment Process*, GAO-11-47 (Washington, D.C.: Oct. 4, 2010).

outstanding investments as of September 30, 2011. Treasury estimates lifetime income of $13 billion for CPP as of September 30, 2011.[16]

Figure 2: Status of CPP, as of September 30, 2011

Capital Purchase Program			
Assets held:	Start date	End date	Approximate exit
Preferred stock with warrants	October 2008	December 2009	Unknown
Subordinated debt with warrants			
Common stock	'08 '09	'10	'11 '12

Dollars in billions		**Estimated lifetime:**	Cost	Income
Status of funding				$13 billion
Highest ever obligated	$204.9			
Disbursed	204.9			
Repayments[a]	182.4			
Write-offs and losses	2.6			
Outstanding investments (book value)	17.3			
Income				
Dividend/interest income	11.2			
Warrant income	7.6			
Proceeds in excess of cost	6.9			
Total income	25.7			
Market value of outstanding investments				
	12.4			

Exit considerations

- The financial strength of CPP participants will determine whether and how quickly institutions can repay and when Treasury can exit.
- Participants' ability to maintain dividend payments to Treasury will affect the estimated lifetime income or cost of the program.
- The dividend rate for some CPP institutions resets beginning in the fall of 2013 and could prompt institutions to repay their investments.
- Treasury currently plans to hold its CPP investments but could change that practice in the future, which could affect the timing of its exit from CPP.

Source: GAO analysis of Treasury data.

[a]The total amount of repayments includes about $400 million from institutions that transferred to CDCI and $2.2 billion from institutions that transferred to the Small Business Lending Fund.

According to data in a Treasury report, nearly half (317) of the 707 institutions that originally participated in CPP had exited the program as of September 30, 2011.[17] Of the 317 institutions that have exited CPP, about 40 percent, or 126 institutions, fully exited by repaying their

---

[16]Throughout this report we use "lifetime income" to refer to instances when cost estimates suggest that certain TARP programs could result in net income for the taxpayer because the proceeds from Treasury's investments (e.g., repayments, dividends, and interest payments) are expected to exceed costs.

[17]See Department of the Treasury, *Troubled Asset Relief Program (TARP) Monthly 105(a) Report-September 2011* (Washington, D.C.: Oct. 11, 2011).

GAO-12-229 Troubled Asset Relief Program

investments.[18] Another 52 percent, or 165 institutions, exited CPP by exchanging their securities under other federal programs: 28 through CDCI and 137 through the Small Business Lending Fund (see fig. 3).[19] Of the remaining 8 percent of CPP recipients that exited the program, 13 went into bankruptcy or receivership, 11 had their securities sold by Treasury, and 2 merged with another institution.

Figure 3: Status of Institutions that Received CPP Investments, as of September 30, 2011

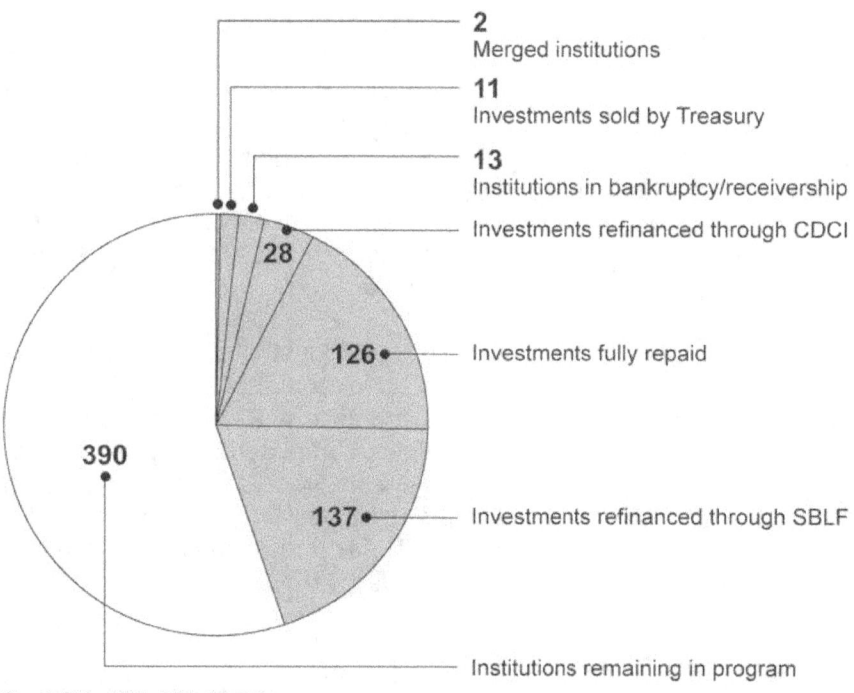

Source: GAO analysis of Treasury data.

---

[18]Additionally, 12 institutions have made partial repayments but remain in the program.

[19]CDCI is a TARP program that provides capital to CDFIs that have a federal depository institution supervisor. The program is structured like CPP but expands to include credit unions and provides more favorable capital terms. The Small Business Lending Fund was created by the Small Business Jobs Act of 2010, Pub. L. No. 111-240, 124 Stat. 2504 (2010), enacted on September 27, 2010. The Fund is a $30 billion capital support program that encourages small and midsize banks and community development loan funds to lend to small businesses.

Also, according to data in a Treasury report, as of September 30, 2011, 390 of the original 707 institutions remained in CPP but accounted for only 8.4 percent of the original investments. Much of the $17.3 billion in outstanding investments was concentrated in a relatively small number of institutions. The largest single outstanding investment was $3.5 billion, and the top four outstanding investments totaled $6.8 billion. The top 25 remaining CPP investments accounted for $11.3 billion.

The cumulative number of financial institutions that had missed at least one scheduled dividend or interest payment by the end of the month in which the payments were due rose from 164 as of November 30, 2010, to 226 as of November 30, 2011.[20] Institutions can elect whether to pay dividends and may choose not to pay for a variety of reasons, including decisions that they or their federal and state regulators make to conserve cash and maintain (or increase) capital levels. Institutions are required to pay dividends only if they declare dividends, although unpaid cumulative dividends generally accrue and the institution must pay them before making payments to other types of shareholders, such as holders of common stock.

These 226 institutions had missed a cumulative total of 1,170 payments.[21] As of November 30, 2011, 184 institutions had missed three or more payments, and 97 had missed six or more. The total amount of missed dividend and interest payments was $429 million, although some of these payments were later made prior to the end of the reporting month. On a quarterly basis, the number of institutions missing dividend or interest payments due on their CPP investments increased steadily from 8 in February 2009 to 158 in November 2011, or about 42 percent of

---

[20]Under CPP terms, institutions pay cumulative dividends on their preferred shares, except for banks that are not subsidiaries of holding companies, which pay noncumulative dividends. Some other types of institutions, such as S corporations, received their CPP investment in the form of subordinated debt and pay Treasury interest rather than dividends. An S-corporation makes a valid election to be taxed under subchapter S of chapter 1 of the Internal Revenue Code and thus does not pay any income taxes. Instead, the corporation's income or losses are divided among and passed through to its shareholders.

[21]These figures differ from the number of dividend or interest payments outstanding because some institutions made their payments after the end of the reporting month. CPP dividend and interest payments are due on February 15, May 15, August 15, and November 15 of each year, or the first business day subsequent to those dates. The reporting period ends on the last day of the calendar month in which the dividend or interest payment is due.

institutions still in the program (see fig. 4).[22] This increase occurred despite reduced program participation, and the proportion of those missing scheduled payments has risen accordingly. The number of institutions missing payments stabilized in recent quarters; however, most of these institutions had repeatedly missed payments. In particular, 119 of the 158 institutions that missed payments in November 2011 had also missed payments in each of the previous three quarters. Moreover, these 158 institutions had missed an average of 4.8 additional previous payments, and only 7 had never missed a previous payment.

Figure 4: Number of Institutions Missing Scheduled Dividend or Interest Payments by Quarter, as of November 30, 2011

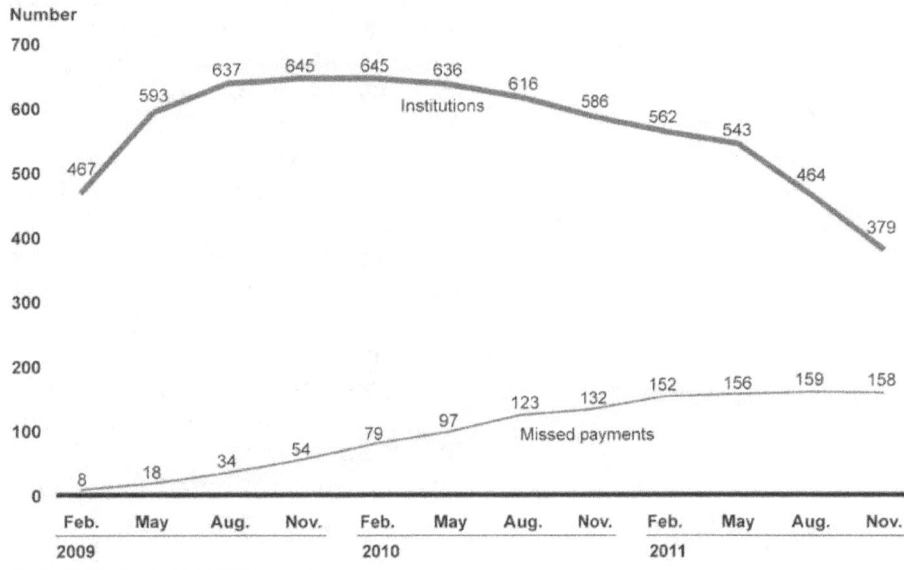

Source: GAO analysis of Treasury data.

Note: Dividend and interest payments are due on a quarterly basis. The number of participating institutions on any given quarter did not reach 707 (i.e., the total number of institutions that participated in CPP) because these institutions entered and exited the programs at different points in time.

---

[22]In its dividend and interest reports, Treasury no longer considers a payment to be missed or unpaid once the institution (1) repays its investment amount and exits CPP, (2) repays dividends by way of capitalization at the time of exchange, or (3) enters bankruptcy or its bank subsidiary is placed into receivership. We included such institutions in our counts.

GAO-12-229 Troubled Asset Relief Program

On July 19, 2011, Treasury announced that it had, for the first time, exercised its right to elect members to the boards of directors of two of the remaining CPP institutions.[23] In considering whether to nominate directors, Treasury said that it would proceed in two steps. First, after an institution misses five dividend or interest payments, Treasury sends OFS staff members to observe board meetings. Second, once an institution has missed six dividend payments, Treasury decides whether to nominate a board member based on a variety of considerations, including what it learns from the board meetings, the institution's financial condition, the function of its board of directors, and the size of its investment.[24]

The financial strength of the participating institutions will largely determine the speed at which institutions repay their investments and exit and the amount of total lifetime income. Institutions will have to demonstrate that they are financially strong enough to repay the CPP investments in order to receive regulatory approval to exit the program. The institutions' financial strength will also be a primary factor in their decisions to make dividend payments, and institutions that continue to miss payments may also have difficulty exiting CPP. Moreover, dividend rates will increase for remaining institutions beginning in late 2013, up to 9 percent, which may prompt institutions to repay their investments as that dividend increase approaches. If broader interest rates are low, especially approaching the dividend reset, banks could have further incentive to redeem their preferred shares. Treasury will need to balance the goals of protecting taxpayer-supported investments while expeditiously unwinding the program. Treasury officials told us that Treasury's practice was generally to hold, rather than sell, its CPP investments.[25] As a result, Treasury's ability to exit the program largely depends on the ability of institutions to

---

[23]According to the standard terms of CPP, after participants have missed six dividend payments—consecutive or not—Treasury can exercise its right to appoint two members to the board of directors for that institution.

[24]Treasury reported that it might not nominate directors immediately after an institution misses six payments but would develop a pool of candidates screened by executive search firms it engaged. Board members whom Treasury nominates cannot be government employees and must have the same fiduciary duties and obligations to the institution's shareholders as any other member of the board and receive the same compensation from the institution.

[25]As noted in figure 3, Treasury has already sold some CPP investments. According to its Section 105(a) reports Treasury may sell its holdings or exchange CPP securities "in limited cases, in order to protect the taxpayers' interest in the value of an investment and to promote the objectives of EESA."

repay their investments. However, Treasury officials noted that if warranted, Treasury could change its practice in the future and sell its investments. In an upcoming report, we plan to describe the financial condition of the remaining CPP institutions and compare them with institutions that already exited and those that never participated.

Financial Strength of CDCI Participants Will Affect When Treasury Exits the Program

Treasury has disbursed $570 million to its 84 CDCI participants, 28 of which had previously participated in CPP (see fig. 5).[26] As we previously reported, CDCI is structured similarly to CPP in that it provides capital to financial institutions by purchasing equity and subordinated debt from them.[27] No additional funds are available through the program, as CDCI's funding authority expired in September 2010. While no CDFIs have repaid Treasury's investment as of September 30, 2011, Treasury has thus far received $10 million in dividend payments from CDCI participants. Lastly, Treasury expects CDCI will cost approximately $182 million over its lifetime, almost a third of the $570 million obligated to the program. Officials stated that CDCI has a cost, while CPP is estimated to result in lifetime income, in part because CDCI provides a lower dividend rate that increases the financing costs. CDCI also does not require warrants of participating institutions, which would otherwise offset Treasury's costs.

---

[26]Institutions interested in transferring to CDCI from CPP were required to be (1) current on dividend payments, (2) in good standing with CPP, and (3) in compliance with all reporting requirements.

[27]While similar to CPP, CDCI differs from CPP in several important aspects: (1) CDCI provides financial assistance to CDFIs, which in turn provide financial services to under-served communities; (2) CDCI also provides assistance to credit unions, unlike CPP; and (3) CDCI provides more favorable capital terms to its participants than CPP, including a longer repayment period at a lower dividend rate. For more details, see GAO-11-74.

Figure 5: Status of CDCI, as of September 30, 2011

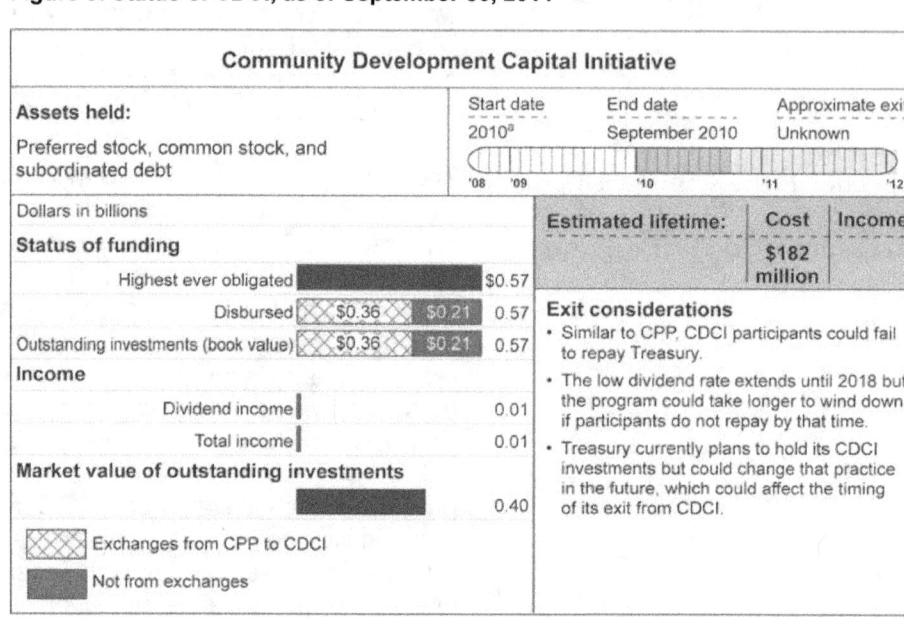

Community Development Capital Initiative

Assets held:	Start date	End date	Approximate exit
Preferred stock, common stock, and subordinated debt	2010[a]	September 2010	Unknown

'08 '09 '10 '11 '12

Dollars in billions

Status of funding

Highest ever obligated	$0.57
Disbursed $0.36 $0.21	0.57
Outstanding investments (book value) $0.36 $0.21	0.57

Income

Dividend income	0.01
Total income	0.01

Market value of outstanding investments

	0.40

Exchanges from CPP to CDCI

Not from exchanges

Estimated lifetime:	Cost	Income
	$182 million	

Exit considerations
- Similar to CPP, CDCI participants could fail to repay Treasury.
- The low dividend rate extends until 2018 but the program could take longer to wind down if participants do not repay by that time.
- Treasury currently plans to hold its CDCI investments but could change that practice in the future, which could affect the timing of its exit from CDCI.

Source: GAO analysis of Treasury data.

[a]Treasury first announced CDCI in October 2009; however, the program first provided capital to CDFIs in 2010.

Note: Treasury began holding common stock for CDCI after September 30, 2011.

As with CPP, Treasury must continue to monitor the performance of CDCI participants because their financial strength will affect their ability to repay Treasury and Treasury's ability to exit the program. As of September 30, 2011, 5 of the 84 CDCI participants had missed at least one dividend or interest payment, according to Treasury. While the continuing weak economy could negatively affect distressed communities and the CDFIs that serve them, the program's low dividend rates may help participants remain current on payments. When Treasury will exit CDCI is unknown but the dividend rate that program participants pay increases in 2018, which provides an incentive for some borrowers to repay before that rate change occurs. As with CPP, Treasury officials indicated that while Treasury's current practice is to hold its CDCI investments, that strategy could change and Treasury could opt to sell its CDCI shares.

Treasury's Balancing of Competing Goals and Market Conditions for AIFP Will Affect the Timing and Outcome of Its Future Exit

Treasury has received more than $40 billion for its roughly $80 billion AIFP investment, in large part from its participation in GM's IPO and its exit from Chrysler. In November and December 2010, Treasury received $13.5 billion from its participation in GM's IPO and $2.1 billion for selling preferred stock in GM. Treasury's investment in Chrysler ended with the repayment of $5.1 billion in loans in May 2011 and the $560 million in proceeds that Treasury received from the sale of its remaining equity stake to Fiat in July 2011. Treasury received $2.7 billion from its sale of Ally Financial trust preferred securities in March 2011.[28]

Treasury's timing of its exit from GM and Ally Financial—and ultimate return on its investment—will depend on how it balances its competing goals of maximizing taxpayer returns and selling its shares as soon as practicable. As figure 6 shows, all of the $37.3 billion in outstanding AIFP funds is from Treasury's investments in GM and Ally Financial, including 32 percent of GM's common stock and 74 percent of Ally Financial's common stock.[29]

---

[28]This amount includes $127 million of proceeds in excess of cost. Ally Financial was formerly known as the General Motors Acceptance Corporation, or GMAC.

[29]If Treasury converted its mandatory convertible preferred securities, its common equity in Ally Financial would increase to more than 80 percent.

Figure 6: Status of AIFP, as of September 30, 2011

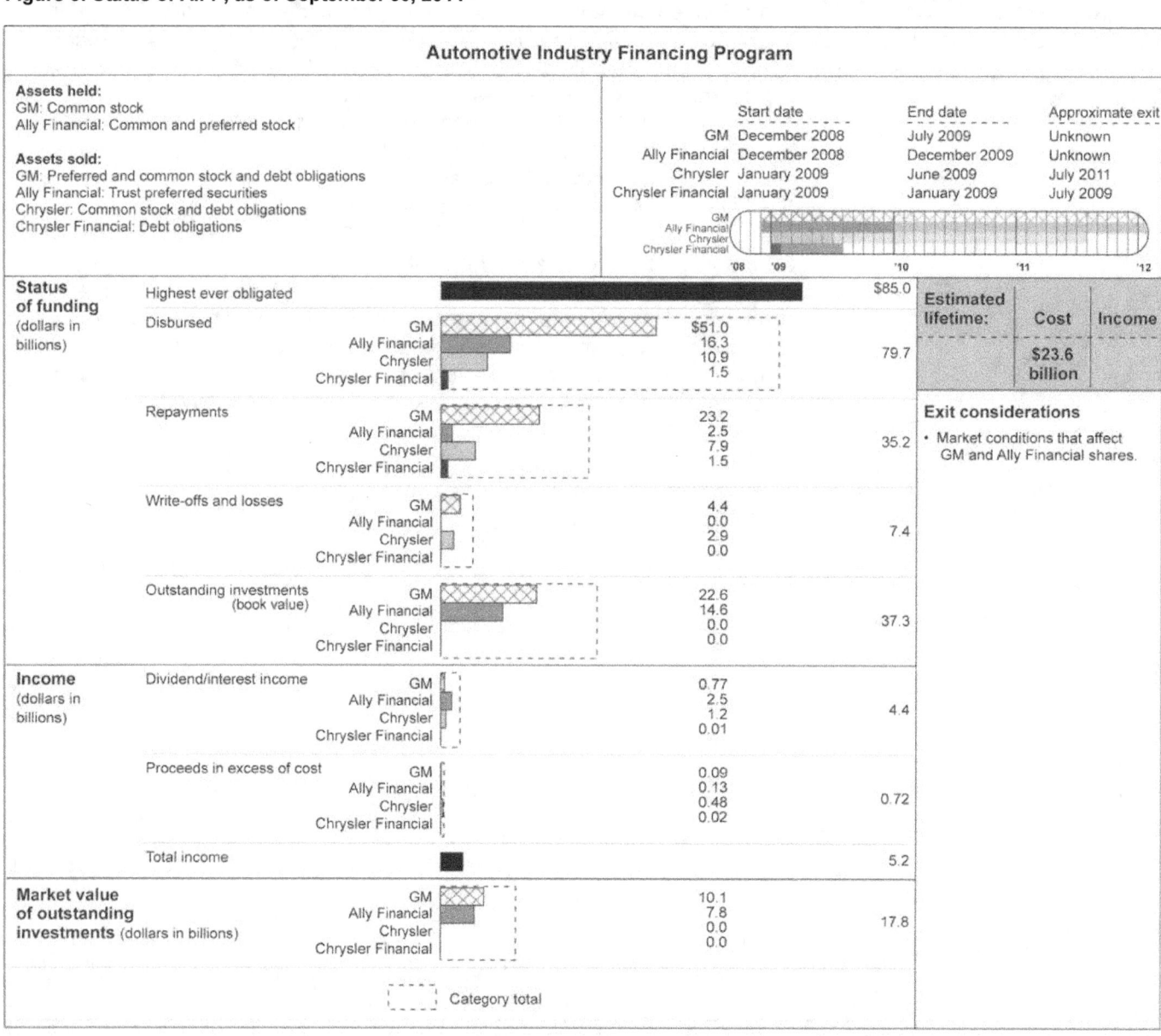

Source: GAO analysis of Treasury data.

Note: Ally Financial was formerly known as the General Motors Acceptance Corporation, or GMAC.

The timing of Ally Financial's IPO will be critical to Treasury's exit strategy, but Ally Financial's mortgage liabilities could hamper the company's efforts to launch an IPO and makes the timing of Treasury's exit from Ally Financial unknown.[30] On March 31, 2011, Ally Financial filed a registration statement with the Securities and Exchange Commission for a proposed IPO but a date has yet to be announced for the IPO. Additionally, after six straight quarterly profits, including growing asset balances for its auto loan business, the company posted a loss of $210 million in the third quarter of 2011, dropping from a profit of about $270 million in the third quarter of 2010, primarily due to losses in its mortgage business. The company attributed these losses to the negative impact of the mortgage servicing rights valuation, resulting from a decline in interest rates and market volatility. Additionally, Ally Financial has $12 billion in debt coming due in 2012.

Treasury officials told us that they continue to monitor market conditions and other factors in determining a divestment strategy for GM, but share prices would have to increase significantly from current levels to fully recoup Treasury's investment in GM. As we previously reported, GM's share price would have to increase by more than 60 percent from the IPO share price of $33 to an average of more than $54 for Treasury to fully recoup its investment.[31] However, over roughly the past year, GM's shares have traded far below the IPO share price—with shares closing above $33 only twice since March 2011, and as of September 30, 2011, the shares closed at $20.18 (fig. 7).

---

[30]Treasury has reported that given that it holds 74 percent of Ally Financial's common equity, it is likely to take 1 to 2 years following the IPO for the Treasury to dispose of its ownership stake. Additionally, Treasury officials have not ruled out the possible sale of its equity but noted that only a small number of institutions could digest an acquisition the size of Ally Financial. Therefore, this course of action appears to be less feasible than an IPO exit strategy.

[31]GAO-11-471. Additional reporting on AIFP appears in GAO, *Troubled Asset Relief Program: Automaker Pension Funding and Multiple Federal Roles Pose Challenges for the Future*, GAO-10-492 (Washington, D.C.: Apr. 6, 2010); *Troubled Asset Relief Program: Continued Stewardship Needed as Treasury Develops Strategies for Monitoring and Divesting Financial Interests in Chrysler and GM*, GAO-10-151 (Washington, D.C.: Nov. 2, 2009); and *Auto Industry: Summary of Government Efforts and Automakers' Restructuring to Date*, GAO-09-553 (Washington, D.C.: Apr. 23, 2009).

Figure 7: GM's Share Price from November 18, 2010, through September 30, 2011, Compared to the IPO Share Price and Post-IPO Share Price Needed to Recoup Treasury's Investment

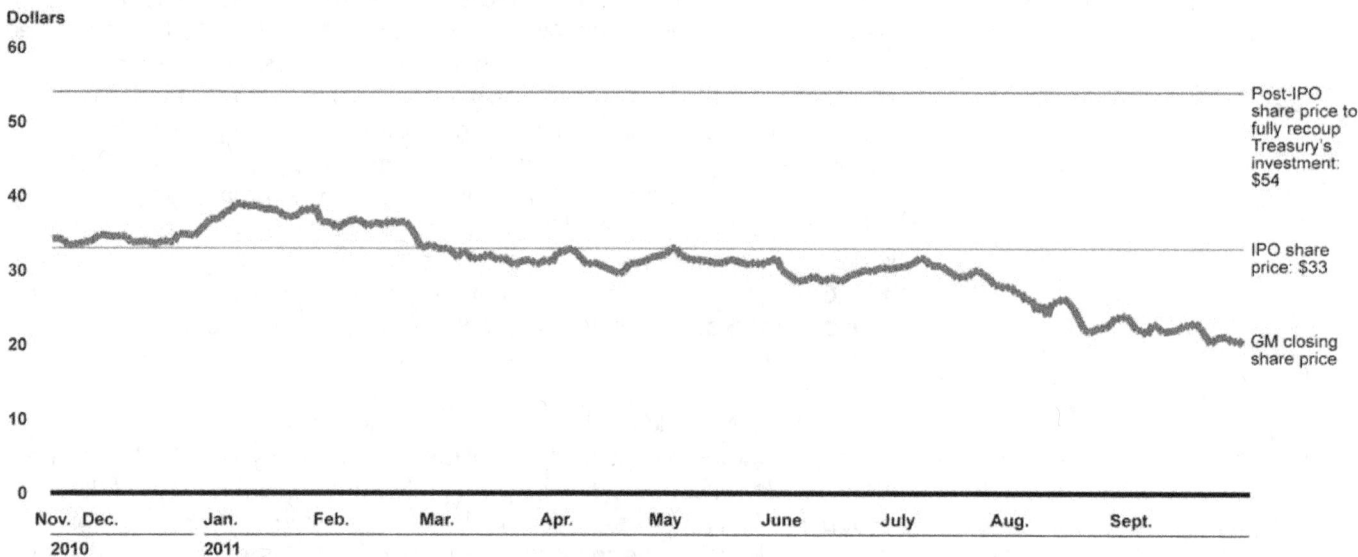

Source: Thomson Reuters Datastream and GAO analysis.

The recent decline in the value of Ally Financial and reductions in the share prices of common stock holdings in GM highlight how market conditions contribute to the risk of AIFP. The projected lifetime cost of AIFP was $23.6 billion as of September 30, 2011, an increase from the $14.7 billion estimate as of September 30, 2010. This change is largely due to the decrease in the trading price of GM's common stock and the decrease in the estimated value of Ally Financial. As Treasury balances its goals of exiting as soon as practicable and maximizing taxpayer returns, it will need to time its divestiture of GM and Ally Financial shares to help recover as much as possible of its investment. Treasury faces the tension of holding shares long enough to potentially recoup its investment, or divesting sooner, likely at a loss.

Treasury's Plans to Sell AIG Shares Are Driven by Market Conditions

In September 2008, prior to TARP, AIG received government assistance in the form of a loan from the Federal Reserve Bank of New York (FRBNY). In exchange, AIG provided shares of preferred stock to the AIG Credit Facility Trust created by FRBNY. These preferred shares were later converted to common stock and transferred to Treasury. In addition to this non-TARP support, Treasury provided TARP assistance to AIG in November 2008 by purchasing preferred shares that were also later converted to common stock. In late January 2011, following the recapitalization of AIG, Treasury owned 1.655 billion TARP and non-TARP common shares in AIG.[32]

Treasury began taking steps in January 2011 to unwind its interest in AIG by conducting the first underwritten offering of its AIG common shares. As we previously reported, Treasury sold 200 million TARP and non-TARP shares in May 2011.[33] Overall, Treasury officials said that Treasury realized a gain because the 200 million shares were sold at $29 per share, which was more than Treasury's overall cost basis of $28.7269 per share.[34] Treasury's 1.455 billion remaining shares after the sale consist of

---

[32]Specifically, in September 2008, a trust created by FRBNY received 100,000 shares of Series C preferred stock and Treasury received a 77.9 percent voting interest in AIG, in exchange for FRBNY providing AIG a revolving loan. This transaction predated TARP. In November 2008, using TARP funds, Treasury purchased $40 billion in cumulative preferred shares of Series D stock, which was exchanged in April 2009 for $41.6 billion of Series E noncumulative preferred stock (the difference of $1.6 billion was in accumulated but unpaid dividends on the Series D stock). That same month, also using TARP funds, Treasury received 300,000 shares of Series F noncumulative preferred stock and a warrant to purchase up to 3,000 shares of AIG common stock in exchange for providing AIG a $29.835 billion equity facility. In January 2011, AIG was recapitalized and Treasury exchanged its Series E and F preferred stock for 1.0921 billion shares of common shares. We refer to these shares as "TARP shares." Also in January, the trust exchanged its Series C preferred stock for 562.9 million shares of common stock and subsequently transferred these shares to Treasury (giving Treasury a total of 1.655 billion common shares in AIG (or approximately 92 percent of the company). We refer to these shares as "non-TARP shares."

[33]The sale included about 132 million TARP AIG common shares on which Treasury had a realized loss and about 68 million non-TARP AIG common shares on which Treasury had a realized gain.

[34]See GAO, Troubled Asset Relief Program: The Government's Exposure to AIG Following the Company's Recapitalization, GAO-11-716 (Washington, D.C.: July 18, 2011). As discussed in GAO-11-716, this calculation is based on a cash-in/cash-out approach and reflects Treasury's primary goal of recouping taxpayers' costs. It includes only the cost of the liquidation preferences in the Series E and Series F preferred shares—$47.543 billion—to calculate a breakeven share price to be $28.73. Under a different approach that captures $47.543 billion of liquidation preferences in Series E and Series F preferred shares plus $1.605 billion of unpaid dividends and fees (for a total of $49.148 billion), the breakeven share price would increase to approximately $29.70, which represents the minimum average price at which Treasury would need to sell all of its shares to fully recover the $49.148 billion. Additional AIG reporting includes GAO, Troubled Asset Relief Program: Third Quarter 2010 Update of Government Assistance Provided to AIG and Description of Recent Execution of Recapitalization Plan, GAO-11-46 (Washington, D.C.: Jan. 20, 2011); Troubled Asset Relief Program: Update of Government Assistance Provided to AIG, GAO-10-475 (Washington, D.C.: Apr. 27, 2010); and Troubled Asset Relief Program: Status of Government Assistance Provided to AIG, GAO-09-975 (Washington, D.C.: Sept. 21, 2009).

960 million TARP and 495 million non-TARP shares. (AIG also sold 100 million shares of common stock during this offering.) The costs for underwriting, Treasury's financial advisors, and Treasury's legal counsel were paid by, and will continue to be paid by, AIG. Treasury, however, pays the costs for assistance it receives from FRBNY. Based on the September 30, 2011, market price of AIG common stock, in selling all of its AIG common shares, Treasury expects to incur a lifetime cost of $24.3 billion for its TARP shares and receive income of $12.8 billion for its non-TARP shares, giving it a lower than expected net estimated cost of $11.5 billion for assistance to AIG (see fig. 8).[35]

---

[35]For example, in March 2010, CBO estimated that the cost of Treasury's approximately $70 billion in TARP assistance (the exchanged Series D/E and F stock mentioned in footnote 34) to AIG would be about $36 billion. Unlike the other lifetime estimates reported here, the lifetime income estimate of $12.8 billion for Treasury's non-TARP shares has not been audited by GAO, although it has been audited. The audited estimate was obtained from the Department of the Treasury, *Agency Financial Report* (Washington, D.C.: Nov. 15, 2011).

Figure 8: Status of AIG Investment Program, as of September 30, 2011

AIG Investment Program		
Assets held: AIG preferred interest (in AIA Aurora LLC special purpose vehicle) AIG common stock	**Assets sold:** AIG preferred interest (in American Life Insurance Company Holdings LLC special purpose vehicle)	Start date: November 2008 End date: n/a Approximate exit: Unknown '08 '09 '10 '11 '12

Dollars in billions

Status of funding

Highest ever obligated	TARP		$69.8
Disbursed TARP (Series D/E)[a]		$40.0	
TARP (Series F)[a]		$27.8	67.8
Non-TARP (Series C)[b]			
Repayments	TARP (Series F)	$11.2	15.0
Write-offs and losses	TARP (Series F)		1.9
Outstanding investments (book value)	TARP	$41.8 $9.3	51.1

Income

Dividend income	TARP	0.25
Other income		0.17
Total income		0.41

Market value of outstanding investments

$21.1 $9.3	30.4

Common   Preferred

Estimated lifetime:	Cost	Income
Non-TARP shares		$12.8 billion
TARP common shares	$24.3 billion	
Net cost	$11.5 billion	

Exit considerations
- Ability of the market to absorb Treasury's shares when it sells.
- Company and external events that could affect the value of AIG stock.
- State of the domestic and global insurance markets.

Source: GAO analysis of Treasury data.

[a] When AIG was recapitalized in January 2011, Treasury exchanged all of its Series E preferred stock and some of its Series F preferred stock into common stock (the remainder of the Series F preferred stock was exchanged for preferred stock in AIA Aurora LLC and American Life Insurance Company Holdings LLC, two special purpose vehicles wholly owned by AIG). As a result of these exchanges, subsequent stock sale, and repayments on the special purpose vehicle preferred stock, Treasury now holds approximately 1.455 billion shares of AIG TARP common stock and about $8.858 billion in AIG TARP preferred interest (the AIA Aurora LLC special purpose vehicle).

[b] During the AIG recapitalization, Treasury also exchanged its Series C shares of non-TARP preferred stock into common stock. Currently, Treasury holds 495 million shares of non-TARP common stock.

AIG originally issued $16 billion of preferred shares in a special purpose vehicle (SPV) called AIA Aurora LLC (or AIA), an SPV created by FRBNY to hold shares of certain portions of AIG's foreign life insurance businesses. Likewise, AIG issued $9 billion of preferred shares in an SPV called American Life Insurance Company (ALICO) Holdings LLC, which was created to hold AIG's ALICO holdings. AIG issued the shares to FRBNY in December 2009 in exchange for a $25 billion reduction in FRBNY's revolving loan to AIG. As part of the recapitalization plan executed on January 14, 2011, AIG redeemed FRBNY's preferred shares by drawing down the Series F equity facility and selling assets. In turn, FRBNY transferred to Treasury the proceeds, along with a cross collateralization agreement against certain other AIG businesses, held for sale. Since the recapitalization, AIG has used the additional sales proceeds to reduce the remaining liquidation preferences of Treasury's preferred interests in the AIA and ALICO SPVs.

Treasury has not announced any time frames for selling its AIG investments, but as it exits this assistance it needs to balance selling its AIG stock as soon as practicable based on market conditions with protecting taxpayers' interests. Treasury officials said that the agency would work to avoid economic losses during this exit. To that end, Treasury officials said that the agency had waited to proceed with its first underwritten offering of AIG common stock until (1) it reacquainted the investment community with AIG and (2) AIG executed and closed other transactions, such as the March 2011 sale of MetLife equity securities and a subsequent March transaction that reduced the preferred interests in the AIA SPV by approximately $5.6 billion.[36] The first underwritten offering of Treasury's AIG common shares occurred in May 2011. Treasury expects to use underwritten offerings to sell most of its common stock in AIG, with assistance from AIG. While Treasury generally prefers to sell the common stock that it holds through underwritten offerings, it could also decide to sell stock through other mechanisms, including more frequent at-the-market offerings.[37]

To sell its AIG stock, officials said that the agency planned to regularly conduct analyses, consider market challenges, and rely on AIG to facilitate Treasury's offerings. Treasury officials have said that they would continue to conduct analyses using factors such as AIG's share price, investor interest in AIG stock, and possible future restructuring. Treasury officials also expect to face several challenges when disposing AIG stock. First, because Treasury owns a significant amount of AIG stock—both as a percentage of total company stock and in absolute terms—the amount of shares the market can absorb may be limited. Second, continued price

---

[36]An "underwritten offering" is a method of issuing shares that targets one or more underwriters, who buy them for their own account and then attempt to sell them to other investors.

[37]An "at-the-market offering" is the sale of securities by an issuer into the public markets at prevailing market prices.

volatility in the domestic and global insurance markets could impede growth in these insurance markets. Third, the continued low interest rate environment could likely lead to lower investment incomes and overall profits for AIG, which in turn could affect Treasury's opportunities to sell its AIG shares. According to Treasury officials, Treasury expects to rely on AIG to prepare and file certain paperwork with the Securities and Exchange Commission and provide other assistance when Treasury sells its remaining AIG shares.[38] Given the decline in AIG's stock price since January 2011 and the recent volatility in the stock market, when Treasury's exit will be completed is unknown. Treasury will also need to balance the tension of its competing goals by deciding whether it should exit even if the stock value is below Treasury's break-even amount.

Treasury Continues Selling SBA 7(a) Securities to Expeditiously Exit Markets

Treasury purchased 31 SBA 7(a) securities between March and September 2010 in an attempt to alleviate liquidity strains in secondary markets for SBA 7(a) loans.[39] Treasury announced in June 2011 that it intended to sell these securities and has sold nearly three-quarters of the portfolio. As of October 2011, Treasury has sold 23 securities. Treasury has eight securities remaining to be sold and projects lifetime income of $3.9 million (see fig. 9).

---

[38]This information is included in the registration rights portion of the December 2010 recapitalization plan.

[39]The SBA 7(a) program is SBA's primary program for assisting small businesses to obtain access to credit when they cannot obtain it from private lending institutions. The program provides credit for working capital and other business needs.

Figure 9: Status of SBA 7(a) Securities Purchase Program, as of September 30, 2011

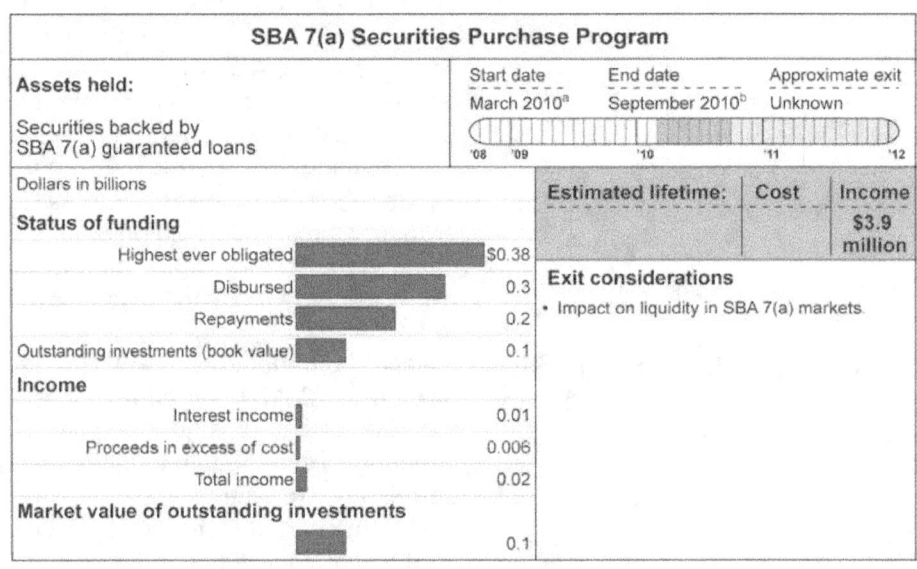

Source: GAO analysis of Treasury data.

Note: This figure represents financial information as of September 30, 2011. It does not include information about securities sold after that date.

[a]The program's first activity was in March 2010, although it was first announced in March 2009.

[b]The program's funding ended in September 2010, though some purchases that were previously committed to prior to September were fulfilled after that date.

Treasury officials took into account market effects when they considered exiting Treasury's portfolio of SBA 7(a) securities. For example, Treasury analyzed SBA lending and securitization volumes, which had recovered to precrisis levels.[40] According to Treasury officials, Treasury also consulted with its external advisor, EARNEST Partners, to understand the potential effect of its sales on the markets. According to Treasury officials, EARNEST Partners advised Treasury that its portfolio was small enough not to affect liquidity in the $15 billion market for SBA 7(a) securities. Moreover, the firm advised Treasury that it had received significant

---

[40]Our previous reporting on SBA 7(a) lending and securitization volumes demonstrated declines during the onset of the financial crisis in 2008, though they recovered from their lows in fiscal year 2010 based on SBA data. See GAO-11-74.

market interest in the securities after Treasury announced its intention to sell them. Treasury officials concluded that it was an opportune time to begin selling these securities without negatively affecting markets.

Treasury officials stated that they considered several tradeoffs in deciding to sell the securities this year, rather than holding them for longer. Exiting quickly appears to be the main consideration, although Treasury officials stated that they balanced this with promoting financial stability and protecting the taxpayer. To determine what prices are reasonable to accept as it continues to sell these securities, Treasury requested market price estimates from two companies for each security it held and compared that to a break-even price and a reserve price, below which it would require additional approvals to proceed with the sale. While Treasury might have maximized taxpayer returns by holding the securities longer, according to Treasury officials, it faced prepayment risk that could have reduced the securities' long-term earning potential.[41]

Treasury Expects Lifetime Income from TALF and to Exit the Program by 2015

The Federal Reserve established TALF to reopen the securitization markets in an effort to improve access to credit for consumers and businesses.[42] Treasury agreed to contribute as much as $4.3 billion to provide credit protection to FRBNY for TALF loans should borrowers neglect to repay and subsequently surrender the asset-backed securities (ABS) or commercial mortgage-backed securities (CMBS) pledged as

---

[41]Prepayment risk is the risk associated with the early, unscheduled return of principal. Because Treasury paid a premium to purchase these securities, any prepayments would result in losses for the amount that Treasury paid in excess of par.

[42]TALF provided loans to certain institutions and business entities in return for collateral in the form of securities that are forfeited if the loans are not repaid. Securitization is a process by which similar debt instruments—such as loans, leases, or receivables—are aggregated into pools, and interest-bearing securities backed by such pools are then sold to investors. These asset-backed securities (ABS) provide a source of liquidity for consumers and small businesses because financial institutions can take assets that they would otherwise hold on their balance sheets, sell them as securities, and use the proceeds to originate new loans, among other purposes. Commercial mortgage-backed securities (CMBS) are securitizations with cash flows backed by principal and interest payments on a pool of loans on commercial properties. For additional information about securitization and about TALF see GAO, *Federal Reserve System: Opportunities Exist to Strengthen Policies and Processes for Managing Emergency Assistance*, GAO-11-696 (Washington, D.C.: July 21, 2011), and *Troubled Asset Relief Program: Treasury Needs to Strengthen Its Decision-Making Process on the Term Asset-Backed Securities Loan Facility*, GAO-10-25 (Washington, D.C.: Feb. 5, 2010).

collateral.[43] To date, Treasury has disbursed $100 million for start up costs related to the TALF SPV, TALF LLC (see fig. 10). This SPV receives a portion of the interest income earned on TALF loans that can be used to purchase any borrower-surrendered collateral from FRBNY, referred to as excess interest.

Figure 10: Status of TALF, as of September 30, 2011

Term Asset-Backed Securities Loan Facility			
Assets held: Asset-backed securities (ABS) and commercial mortgage-backed securities (CMBS)	Start date March 2009[a]	End date June 2010	Approximate exit 2015

Dollars in billions		Estimated lifetime:	Cost	Income
Status of funding				$421 million
Highest ever obligated	$20.0			
Disbursed	0.1	**Exit considerations**		
Outstanding investments (book value)[b]	0.1	• Fluctuations in CMBS risks and valuations could affect Treasury's ultimate returns on TALF.		
Income				
Total income	0.0	**Current loan balance**		
Market value of outstanding investments[b]	0.6	$11.3 billion outstanding / $59.7 billion repaid	$71 billion total	

Source: GAO analysis of Treasury data.

[a]Although the program was first announced in November 2008, the first program activity was initiated in March 2009.

[b]The book value of Treasury's outstanding investments is the same as the $100 million contributed by Treasury to the TALF SPV. The market value of Treasury's outstanding investments is the net book value for the $100 million TALF contribution calculated using Credit Reform Accounting.

FRBNY stopped issuing new TALF loans in 2010.[44] Treasury officials report that FRBNY TALF loan balances have fallen from $29.7 billion in September 2010 to $11.3 billion as of September 30, 2011. Agency

---

[43]Initially, Treasury was responsible for providing as much as $20 billion in credit protection to FRBNY, but in July 2010, Treasury and the Federal Reserve agreed to reduce the credit protection to $4.3 billion.

[44]TALF expired on March 31, 2010, for loans backed by ABS and legacy CMBS, and on June 30, 2010, for loans backed by newly issued CMBS.

officials also indicated that all TALF loans are current and borrowers continue to pay down their loans.

The excess interest in TALF LLC grew by more than 30 percent between October 2010 and September 2011, from $523 million to $685.6 million. As a result, if the TALF LLC balance exceeds the value of any surrendered collateral, Treasury may not need to disburse any additional funds for the program and could instead realize lifetime income, given that it will receive 90 percent of funds remaining in TALF LLC after loans are repaid and the program ends. In addition, the equity that borrowers hold in TALF collateral has grown since TALF loans were first issued.[45] As of September 30, 2011, Treasury expects that TALF will result in lifetime income of $421 million. Despite these positive trends, FRBNY and Treasury staff continue to monitor market conditions and credit rating agency actions that could affect TALF assets. Moreover, as we have previously reported, market value fluctuations could affect future results. In particular, continued volatility in global markets could be reflected in CMBS pricing because, according to Treasury officials, CMBS has exhibited greater correlation with investor sentiment and broad volatility in other risk assets versus other types of ABS.

Treasury expects to exit TALF by 2015, although it does not have complete control over its exit because its role in TALF is secondary to that of the Federal Reserve. Treasury models loan repayments using TALF loan terms and data provided by the Federal Reserve and projects repayment schedules, collateral cash flows, prepayments, and performance loss rates. Based on these analyses, Treasury expects that the last TALF loan will be due in 2015. However, should any assets be surrendered to TALF LLC, Treasury could be involved in TALF beyond that date as it may be required to lend to TALF LLC to purchase and manage assets until they are sold or reach maturity.

---

[45]The FRBNY establishes the "haircut" or amount of equity the borrower holds in TALF collateral based on its weighted average life and market risks for each sector and sub sector. The haircut is also the difference between the value of the TALF collateral and the value of the loan. In other words, if haircuts have grown, the borrower has more equity in the collateral and should be more likely to pay off the loan and keep the pledged collateral. See GAO-10-25 for more details.

Remaining PPIP Funds Continue to Invest, Although One Fund Is Unwinding Prior to Expected End Date

Treasury created PPIP, partnering with private funds, to purchase troubled mortgage-related assets from financial institutions. PPIFs are in their 3-year investment period, which starts at a fund's inception date. There were nine PPIFs established through PPIP.[46] The investment period ends for each of the remaining PPIFs between October and December 2012, at which time the PPIFs can no longer draw money from Treasury or make new investments.[47] Once the investment period ends, PPIFs must begin the process of unwinding their positions and must completely divest within 5 years—although Treasury can decide to extend this period for up to two additional years for each PPIF. One fund notified Treasury in September 2011 that it terminated its investment period and therefore will no longer actively invest. Therefore, this fund has begun to unwind.

According to Treasury, PPIFs have accessed about 80 percent of the equity and debt available through Treasury and private investors as of September 30, 2011, and have repaid a total of $1.2 billion in debt financing as of September 30, 2011. Treasury estimates that PPIP will ultimately result in lifetime income of about $2.4 billion (see fig. 11). However, the ultimate results will depend on a variety of factors, including when PPIFs choose to divest and the performance of the assets they hold.

---

[46]One PPIF liquidated in the first quarter of 2010.

[47]PPIFs received an approximately equal share of equity from Treasury and private investors. PPIFs also received access to credit from Treasury. PPIFs draw on these funds to invest in eligible RMBS and CMBS.

Figure 11: Status of PPIP, as of September 30, 2011

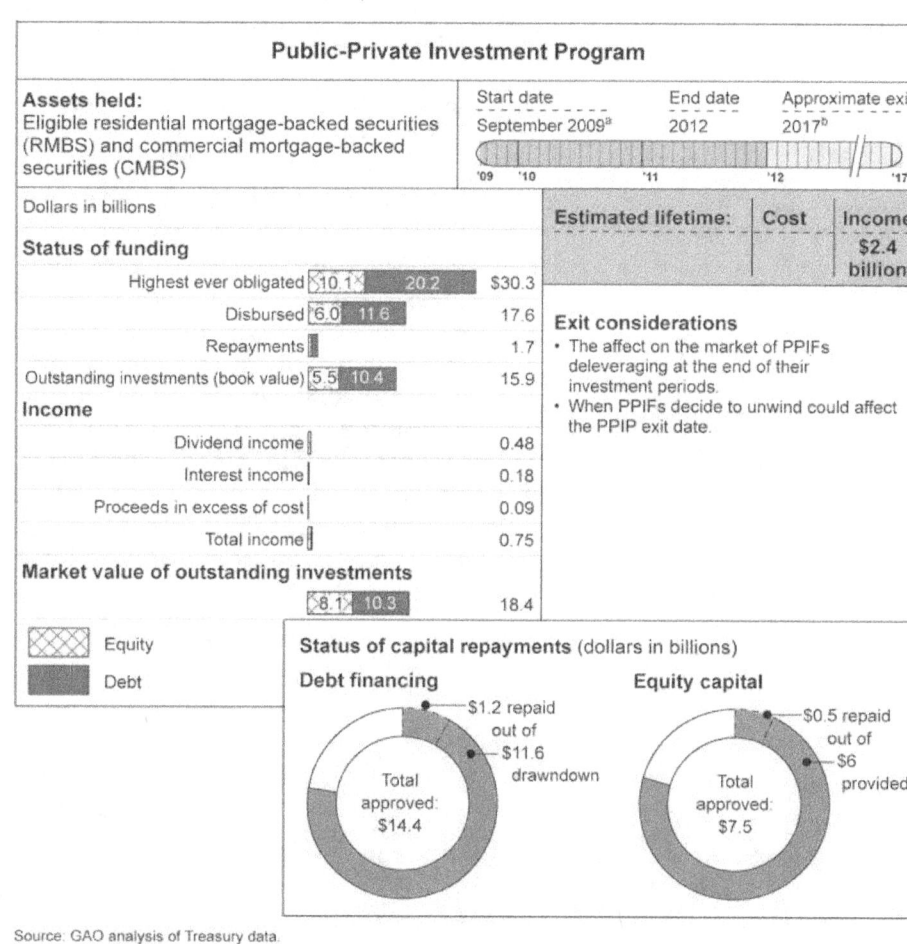

Public-Private Investment Program

Assets held:	Start date	End date	Approximate exit
Eligible residential mortgage-backed securities (RMBS) and commercial mortgage-backed securities (CMBS)	September 2009[a]	2012	2017[b]

Dollars in billions

	Estimated lifetime:	Cost	Income
			$2.4 billion

Status of funding

Highest ever obligated	10.1 / 20.2	$30.3
Disbursed	6.0 / 11.6	17.6
Repayments		1.7
Outstanding investments (book value)	5.5 / 10.4	15.9

Income

Dividend income	0.48
Interest income	0.18
Proceeds in excess of cost	0.09
Total income	0.75

Market value of outstanding investments

8.1 / 10.3	18.4

Exit considerations
- The affect on the market of PPIFs deleveraging at the end of their investment periods.
- When PPIFs decide to unwind could affect the PPIP exit date.

Equity

Debt

Status of capital repayments (dollars in billions)

Debt financing
$1.2 repaid out of $11.6 drawndown
Total approved: $14.4

Equity capital
$0.5 repaid out of $6 provided
Total approved: $7.5

Source: GAO analysis of Treasury data.

[a]PPIFs began their investment periods in 2009. Active PPIFs will continue to invest until the investment period ends in 2012. The program was first announced in March 2009.

[b]The stipulated exit date is 2017, though the program could be extended through 2019.

While PPIFs are in the investment period, Treasury officials said that their role is to follow the progress of each PPIF's investment strategy, the risks being taken in each portfolio, and the target returns for each portfolio. In this role, Treasury staff and contractors monitor compliance with PPIP terms. Also, Treasury has hired a contractor to provide investment fund consulting and analysis of PPIF portfolios.

GAO-12-229 Troubled Asset Relief Program

Current PPIP terms stipulate an exit by 2017.[48] Unlike some other TARP programs, Treasury officials do not face the same consideration of competing goals in exiting the program, given that the terms of the program dictate when the PPIFs must wind down. However, Treasury officials noted that PPIFs can liquidate at any time. Given that one PPIF has chosen to end its investments as of September 30, 2011, it is possible that if others follow the program could end sooner than estimated. Such action by PPIFs would affect Treasury's estimates for future income from the program when it ends. Officials also noted that the program was designed to encourage firms to deleverage after the investment period, at which time PPIFs would no longer have access to debt financing from Treasury. Once the investment period concludes, the PPIFs can no longer access funds from Treasury and must pay down the Treasury loan and make distributions to the partners as RMBS and CMBS are sold. Officials noted that this program structure creates an incentive for PPIFs to sell their assets promptly once their access to Treasury credit ends. Treasury officials noted that they were not concerned about the effect of PPIP's eventual wind down on markets, as the 5-year period for unwinding would likely mitigate any potential impact.

[48]While PPIP is scheduled to end in 2017, which is 8 years after the last PPIP was initiated, it could be extended for 2 years. Such decisions would occur on a case-by-case basis for each PPIF, depending on market conditions and other factors.

Unlike Most Other Programs, TARP-Funded Housing Programs Remain Ongoing and Represent Direct Outlays of TARP Funds

To help meet EESA's goals of preventing avoidable foreclosures and preserving homeownership, Treasury has allocated $45.6 billion in TARP funds to three programs: Making Home Affordable (MHA), which has several components; Hardest Hit Fund (HHF); and the Department of Housing and Urban Development's Federal Housing Administration (FHA) Short Refinance Program (see fig. 12). Treasury could potentially disburse TARP funds under these three programs for several more years—until September 2020 in the case of the FHA Short Refinance program. Unlike other TARP-funded programs, the expenditures under these three housing programs are direct outlays of funds with no provision for repayment. Given these characteristics, Treasury does not face the same tension between exiting programs as soon as practicable and maximizing taxpayer returns as it does with some other TARP programs.

Figure 12: TARP-funded Housing Programs, Amounts Obligated and Disbursed, and Reported Activity through September 2011

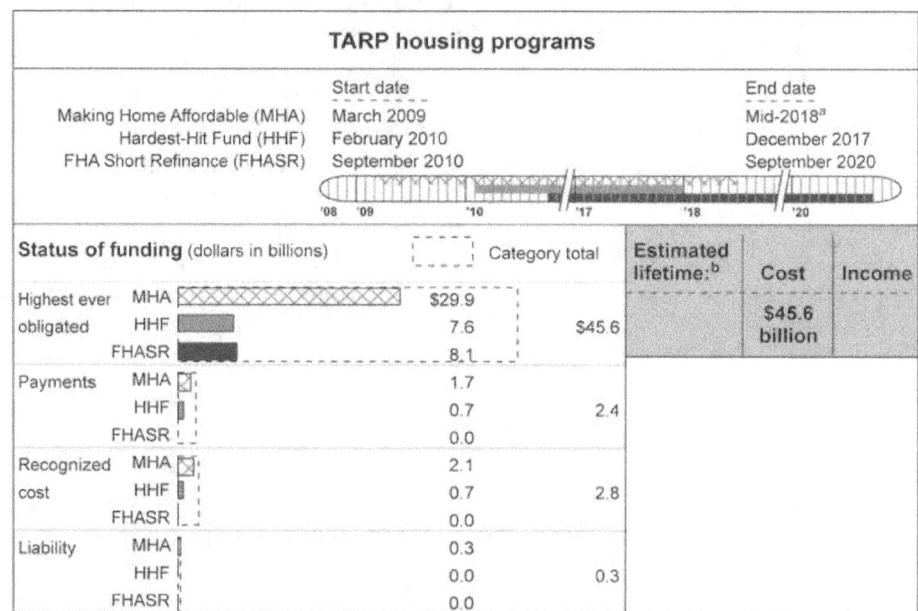

TARP housing programs		
	Start date	End date
Making Home Affordable (MHA)	March 2009	Mid-2018[a]
Hardest-Hit Fund (HHF)	February 2010	December 2017
FHA Short Refinance (FHASR)	September 2010	September 2020

Status of funding (dollars in billions)			Category total	Estimated lifetime:[b]	Cost	Income
Highest ever obligated	MHA	$29.9			$45.6 billion	
	HHF	7.6	$45.6			
	FHASR	8.1				
Payments	MHA	1.7				
	HHF	0.7	2.4			
	FHASR	0.0				
Recognized cost	MHA	2.1				
	HHF	0.7	2.8			
	FHASR	0.0				
Liability	MHA	0.3				
	HHF	0.0	0.3			
	FHASR	0.0				

Reported activity through September 2011 by subcomponent (if applicable)

MHA	Home Affordable Modification Program (HAMP)	856,974 HAMP permanent modifications
	Home Price Decline Protection Incentives	83,028 modifications
	Home Affordable Foreclosure Alternatives (HAFA) Program	18,557 HAFA agreements completed
	Second Lien Modification Program (2MP)	45,705 2MP modifications
	Principal Reduction Alternative (PRA)	29,342 PRA permanent modifications
	Government Loans (FHA and Department of Agriculture Rural Housing Service HAMP (RD-HAMP) loan modifications)	4,671 FHA-HAMP modifications / No RD-HAMP modification yet reported
	Treasury/FHA Second Lien Program (FHA2LP)	No activity reported
HHF		19,025 HFA borrowers assisted
FHASR		334 FHA loans refinanced

Source: GAO analysis of Treasury data.

[a]Borrowers have until December 31, 2012, to accept their trial period plan for HAMP by making a timely first trial payment. Trial modifications must be successful for at least 3 months before borrowers can convert into a permanent modification. Incentive payments can be made for up to 5 years after the date of conversion from a trial modification. Additionally, servicers can take several months before submitting loan data for incentive payments. As a result, Treasury officials estimated that the last HAMP incentive payment would likely occur sometime in mid-2018.

[b]Treasury's estimated lifetime cost estimates reflect the actual outlay of funds to the housing programs and do not utilize the same credit reform accounting as the other program-specific lifetime cost estimates.

The centerpiece of Treasury's MHA program is HAMP, which seeks to help eligible borrowers facing financial distress avoid foreclosure by reducing their monthly first lien mortgage payments to more affordable levels (31 percent of their monthly income).[49] Treasury announced HAMP on February 18, 2009. Borrowers have until December 31, 2012, to accept an offered trial period plan by making a timely first trial period payment. Under HAMP, Treasury shares the cost of lowering borrowers' monthly payments from 38 to 31 percent of monthly income for a 5-year period with the mortgage holder or investors. Treasury also provides a series of incentive payments to servicers, investors, and borrowers if specific program conditions are met. Treasury originally announced that up to 3 to 4 million borrowers would be helped under HAMP.[50] Through September 2011, Treasury reported that 856,974 permanent modifications had been started and, as shown in figure 13, monthly activity to date peaked during the early part of 2010.[51] These results likely reflect Treasury's decision to require all servicers starting on June 1, 2010, to perform full verification of borrower's eligibility for HAMP before initiating a trial modification (previously servicers were allowed to offer trial modifications using unverified information provided by the borrower). Monthly trial modification starts during September 2011 were the lowest reported since January 2010. Treasury recently announced that it had launched a nationwide advertisement campaign to increase awareness of the MHA program among eligible homeowners.

---

[49]To be eligible for HAMP: (1) the property must be owner occupied and the borrower's primary residence; (2) the property must be a single-family property (one to four units) with a maximum unpaid principal balance on the unmodified first lien mortgage that is equal to or less than $729,750 for a one-unit property; (3) the loan must have been originated on or before January 1, 2009; and (4) the monthly first lien mortgage payment must be more than 31 percent of the homeowner's gross monthly income.

[50]We have made a number of recommendations to Treasury regarding its efforts to implement the MHA program. See GAO-11-288; Troubled Asset Relief Program: Further Actions Needed to Fully and Equitably Implement Foreclosure Mitigation Programs, GAO-10-634 (Washington, D.C.: June 24, 2010); and Troubled Asset Relief Program: Treasury Actions Needed to Make the Home Affordable Modification Program More Transparent and Accountable, GAO-09-837 (Washington, D.C: July 23, 2009). While Treasury has taken various actions consistent with our recommendations, several of our MHA-related recommendations remain open. See GAO, Troubled Asset Relief Program: Status of GAO Recommendations to Treasury, GAO-11-906R (Washington, D.C.: Sept. 16, 2011).

[51]Under HAMP, borrowers must successfully complete a trial modification of at least 3 months (90 days) before receiving a permanent modification.

Figure 13: HAMP Modifications Started Monthly from January 2010 through September 2011

Borrowers in thousands

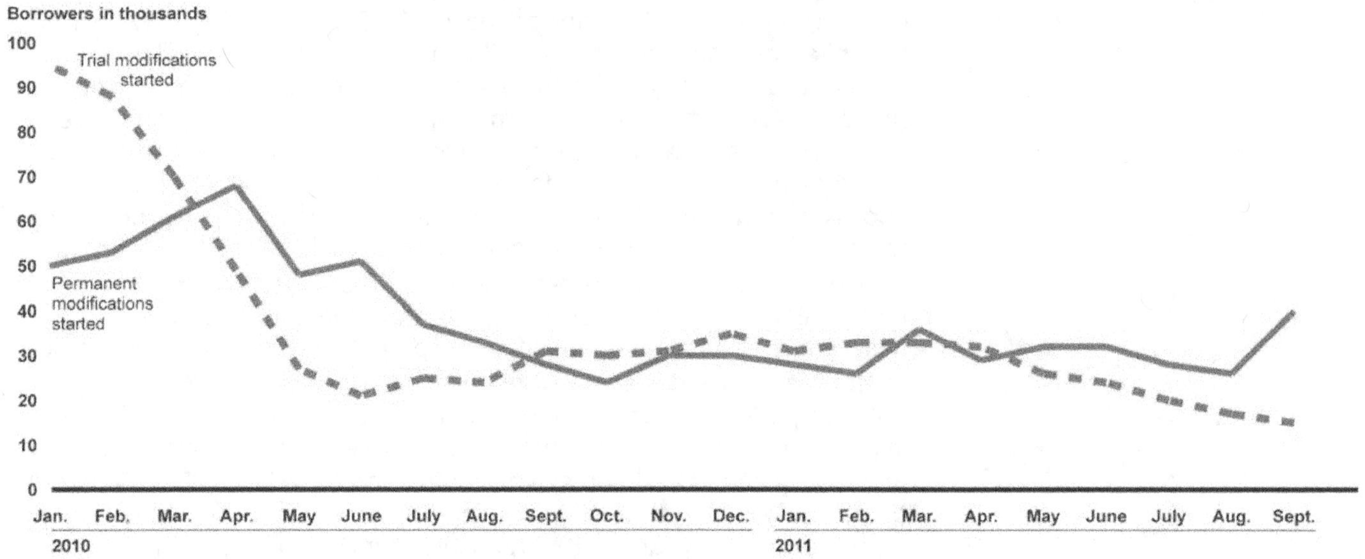

Source: GAO analysis of Treasury data.

In addition to HAMP, Treasury has implemented a number of additional MHA components that use TARP funds to augment or complement the HAMP first lien modification program:[52]

- *Home Affordable Foreclosure Alternatives Program.* The Home Affordable Foreclosure Alternatives Program offers assistance to homeowners looking to exit their homes through a short sale or deed-in-lieu of foreclosure. Treasury offers incentives to eligible homeowners, servicers, and investors under the program. Through September 2011, servicers reported completing 18,043 short sales and 514 deeds-in-lieu under the program.

---

[52]Treasury's MHA program also has the Home Affordable Unemployment Program that does not entail the use of TARP or other federal program funds. The Unemployment Program provides temporary forbearance to homeowners who are unemployed and requires servicers participating in MHA to grant qualified unemployed borrowers a forbearance period during which their mortgage payments are temporarily reduced or suspended for a minimum of 12 months while they look for new jobs. Borrowers can apply for a HAMP modification upon finding employment or prior to the expiration of the forbearance period. Treasury reported that 14,996 Unemployment Program forbearance plans had been started through August 2011.

GAO-12-229 Troubled Asset Relief Program

- *Home Price Decline Protection Incentives.* Home Price Decline Protection Incentives provides investors with additional incentives for HAMP modifications of loans on properties located in areas where home prices have recently declined and where investors are concerned that price declines may persist. Through September 2011, Treasury has paid about $135 million to investors in program incentives to support the HAMP modification of 83,028 loans.

- *Principal Reduction Alternative (PRA).* PRA requires servicers of nongovernment sponsored enterprise loans to evaluate the benefit of principal reduction for mortgages with a loan-to-value ratio of 115 percent or greater when evaluating a homeowner for a HAMP first lien modification. While servicers are required to evaluate homeowners for PRA, they are not required to reduce principal as part of the modification. PRA can be a component of a HAMP trial or permanent modification. Through September 2011, servicers reported having started 29,342 permanent modifications that had the principal reduced under PRA.

- *Second Lien Modification Program.* The Second Lien Modification Program provides additional assistance to homeowners receiving a HAMP first lien permanent modification who have an eligible second lien with participating servicers. When a borrower's first lien is modified under HAMP, participating program servicers must offer to modify the borrower's eligible second lien according to a defined protocol.[53] This assistance can result in a modification or even full or partial extinguishment of the second lien. Through September 2011, servicers reported starting 45,705 second lien modifications, of which 6,332 had the second lien fully extinguished.

- *Government loans (FHA- and RD-HAMP).* FHA and the Department of Agriculture's Rural Housing Services (RHS) have implemented programs to modify FHA-insured or RHS-guaranteed first lien mortgage loans in a manner complementary to HAMP. Each of these programs provides a borrower with an affordable monthly mortgage payment equal to 31 percent of his or her monthly gross income and

---

[53]In order to be eligible for a Second Lien Modification Program modification, the loan must meet certain criteria. For example, it must have been originated on or before January 1, 2009; have an unpaid balance of greater than $5,000 and have a premodification monthly payment greater than $100; and can be modified only once under the program.

requires the borrower to complete a trial payment plan before the loan is permanently modified. If the modified FHA-insured or RHS-guaranteed mortgage loan meets Treasury's eligibility criteria, the borrower and servicer can receive TARP-funded incentive payments from Treasury. Treasury reported that there were 4,671 permanent FHA-HAMP modifications that had been started through September 2011. According to Treasury officials, servicers have not reported any activity for the Rural Development (RD)-HAMP program as of September 30, 2011.

- *Treasury/FHA Second Lien Program (FHA2LP).* Under this program, Treasury will provide incentive payments to servicers and investors if they partially or fully extinguish second liens associated with an FHA Short Refinance. According to Treasury officials, no second liens have been extinguished, and no incentive payments have been made under the Treasury/FHA Second Lien Program as of September 30, 2011.

To facilitate this refinance opportunity, Treasury will provide incentives under its TARP-funded FHA2LP to servicers and investors that partially or fully extinguish second liens associated with an FHA Short Refinance. Servicers can receive a one-time payment of $500 for each second lien extinguished under the program and investors are eligible for incentive payments based on the amount of principal extinguished. According to Treasury officials, servicers have reported no activity under FHA2LP as of September 30, 2011.

In addition to the MHA program, Treasury has allocated $7.6 billion in TARP funds for the Hardest Hit Fund (HHF), which seeks to help homeowners in the states hit hardest by unemployment and house price declines: Alabama, Arizona, California, Florida, Georgia, Illinois, Indiana, Kentucky, Michigan, Mississippi, Nevada, New Jersey, North Carolina, Ohio, Oregon, Rhode Island, South Carolina, and Tennessee plus the District of Columbia. States were chosen because they have experienced either steep home price declines or high levels of unemployment in the economic downturn. According to Treasury, each state housing agency gathered public input to implement programs designed to meet the distinct challenges homeowners in their state were facing. As a result, HHF programs vary across states, but services offered often include mortgage payment assistance for unemployed homeowners and reinstatement assistance to cover arrearages (e.g., one-time payment to bring a borrower's delinquent mortgage current). According to Treasury, it paid approximately $700 million to the states for the HHF program as of the end of September 2011 and the states reported having helped about 19,025 homeowners during this approximate time period.

Treasury has also allocated $8.1 billion in TARP funds to the FHA Short Refinance program to enable homeowners whose mortgages exceed the value of their homes to refinance into more affordable mortgages. This opportunity allows borrowers who are current on their mortgage to qualify for an FHA Short Refinance loan provided that the lender or investor writes off the unpaid principal balance of the original first lien mortgage by at least 10 percent. Treasury entered into a letter of credit facility with Citibank in order to fund up to $8 billion of losses, if any, associated with providing FHA Short Refinance loans originated on or before December 31, 2012. Treasury's commitment extends until September 2020, and to the extent that FHA experiences losses on those refinanced mortgage loans, Treasury will pay claims up to the predetermined percentage after the FHA has paid its portion of the claim. Treasury will also pay a fee to the issuer of the letter of credit based on the amount of funds drawn against the letter of credit and any unused amount. Treasury has estimated that the letter of credit fee will be $55 million over the life of the program. As of August 31, 2011, FHA had guaranteed 334 loans with a total face value of $73 million under the refinance program. No defaults had occurred on these guarantees to date. As of August 31, 2011, Treasury has paid a total of $4.9 million to Citibank ($1.9 million during fiscal year 2011) in fees as the letter of credit issuer.

Treasury Continues to Address Staffing Needs While Also Relying on Financial Agents and Contractors to Support TARP Administration and Programs

OFS Staffing Declined Slightly for the First Time and Treasury Is Addressing Turnover-Related Staffing Issues

As we have identified in previous reports, Treasury still faces staffing challenges, including recent turnover stemming from the departure of term-appointed staff, but it has been addressing these challenges. Overall staffing numbers steadily increased from 2008 through 2010 but began declining for the first time in 2011 (see fig. 14).

Figure 14: OFS Employees and Detailees, November 21, 2008, through September 30, 2011

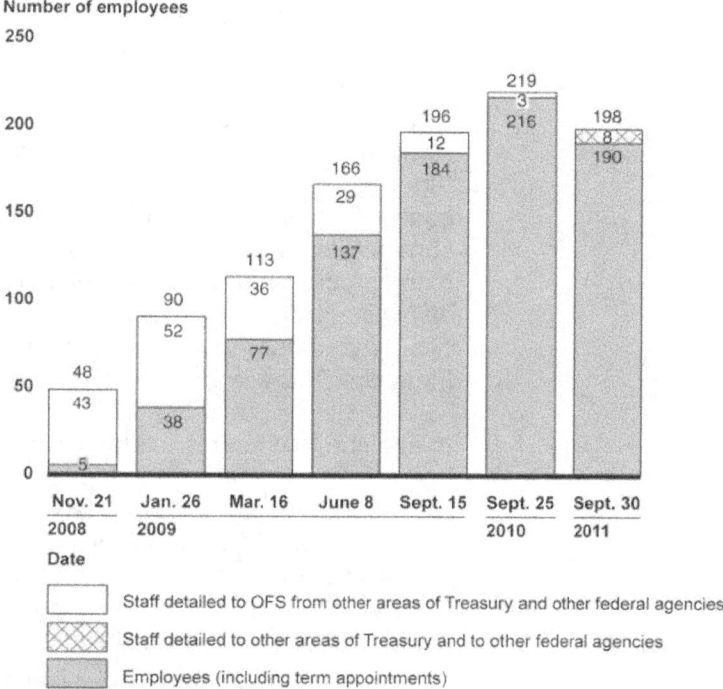

Number of employees

Staff detailed to OFS from other areas of Treasury and other federal agencies

Staff detailed to other areas of Treasury and to other federal agencies

Employees (including term appointments)

Source: GAO analysis of Treasury data.

Also, as we previously reported in September 2011, OFS no longer has detailees from other federal agencies. When OFS was first organized, it relied on a significant number of staff from other agencies to start up new TARP programs. With most TARP programs winding down, OFS officials stated that OFS has begun to detail OFS staff to other Treasury programs, such as the Small Business Lending Fund (SBLF), and other federal agencies, such as the Bureau of Consumer Financial Protection. From September 2010 through September 2011, about 65 staff left OFS, according to Treasury officials.

As overall staffing numbers have declined, staffing levels within individual OFS offices have fluctuated depending on staffing needs. In some offices, for instance, staff levels have decreased. For example, in the Chief Investment Office—which includes staff working on various TARP programs, such as CPP—more than half of the staff departed from June 2010 to September 2011 (a decrease of 20 staff from 2010). Though some Chief Investment Office staff were replaced with staff in other OFS offices and staff that were new to Treasury, many were not replaced because their skill sets were no longer needed given the wind-down phase of investment programs. Conversely, staff have increased in certain OFS offices where OFS management had identified specific needs. For example, the number of staff in the Office of Internal Review (OIR), which identifies risks and develops procedures for complying with EESA, increased from June 2010 to September 2011. Treasury had been seeking new staff with the skill set needed for this work, as we previously reported, and officials stated that the increase reflected a need to continue monitoring compliance among Treasury financial agents and contractors. Treasury filled these positions in part by streamlining the hiring process and better targeting its job announcements. Treasury officials anticipate that staffing levels in most OFS offices will decrease over time, though it will continue to seek talent for OIR, the Chief Financial Office, and the TARP housing programs that remain active.

In addition to changes in staff numbers and office composition, OFS has had a number of its leadership team depart since 2010. As we previously reported, the Assistant Secretary of Financial Stability resigned on September 30, 2010. His replacement is OFS's former Chief Counsel, who was sworn in as Assistant Secretary in July 2011. An acting Chief Counsel has assumed the Assistant Secretary's former role. Other staff in leadership positions have resigned since we last reported in January 2011. The Chief Investment Officer and the Chief of Operations both left OFS and were replaced internally by OFS staff members. Both of these departing staff were in 3-year term senior executive service positions that were set to expire, according to Treasury officials. The Chief of Operations position is now held by a permanent staff member in an acting capacity, while the Chief Investment Officer position remains a term position. Program leadership has also changed for Treasury's first and largest program, CPP. Its director left Treasury in 2011 and was replaced with another staff member from the Chief Investment Office.

Though OFS has experienced staff turnover and still faces staffing challenges, OFS has been addressing these and other staffing issues. For example:

- As we previously reported, we recommended that OFS finalize its staffing plan. Treasury has implemented this recommendation, which should help OFS better ensure that it recognizes and addresses its staffing challenges, given that many staff still remain in term appointments.[54] As a result of this plan, OFS produced information on critical positions that should remain or be filled and successors for all of the chiefs and those in critical management positions directly below the chief level. OFS also plans to conduct succession planning for other staff below the management level.

- OFS now hires predominantly term-appointed staff for a maximum of 2 years, according to Treasury officials. Previously, it hired staff for "permanent" positions as well as term-appointed positions with a maximum of 4 years. Treasury officials noted that they made this change in recognition of the fact that most of its programs are winding down. Additionally, limiting new hires to shorter-term appointments reduces the number of staff that Treasury will need to absorb when OFS closes.

- OFS has also filled or removed a number of vacancies to recognize that it is in a period of winding down. Specifically, OFS vacancies decreased from 61 in 2010 to 29 as of September 30, 2011.

In addition, OFS continues to address employee morale concerns. As we previously reported, an employee survey in 2010 identified communication and staff development as two areas for improvement. According to Treasury officials, OFS took steps to address communication concerns through a monthly newsletter; "lunch and learn" sessions on a variety of topics; and briefings attended by senior Treasury officials, such as the Secretary of the Treasury. To address concerns about staff development, OFS officials said that they increased training offerings and provided the opportunity to complete professional development plans. Treasury has also been assisting term-appointed staff. For example, Treasury officials stated that they have continued to provide information sessions for those staff on term appointments that are seeking permanent positions in the federal government. Officials also noted that they have briefings on helping staff in term appointments understand the terms of the appointment and to find opportunities for detail positions to other agencies.

---

[54]See GAO-11-906R for more information.

Treasury Increased Its Use of Financial Agents and Contractors

Treasury continues to rely heavily on financial agents to support TARP programs. According to OFS procedures, financial agency agreements are used for services that cannot be provided with existing Treasury or contractor resources and generally involve inherently governmental functions. Since the start of TARP, Treasury has relied on financial agents for asset management, transaction structuring, disposition services, custodial services, and administration and compliance support for the TARP housing assistance programs. Through fiscal year 2011, Treasury awarded 17 financial agency agreements, of which 14 remain active. As shown in table 2, the total obligated value of financial agency agreements increased from about $327 million to about $547 million, or 67 percent, from the end of fiscal year 2010 to the end of fiscal year 2011. Treasury awarded two new financial agency agreements in fiscal year 2011 for transaction structuring and disposition services.

Table 2: Contracts and Financial Agency Agreements in Support of TARP, Fiscal Years 2010 through 2011

	Obligated value through fiscal year 2010	Obligated value[a] through fiscal year 2011	Increase from fiscal years 2010 through 2011	
Financial agency agreements	$327,355,188	$547,487,042	$220,131,854	67%
Contracts	108,907,207	154,934,812	46,027,605	42
Total	**$436,262,395**	**$702,421,854**	**$266,159,459**	**61%**

Source: GAO analysis of Treasury data.

[a]Obligated value generally includes obligations from the beginning of TARP through the end of the fiscal year, according to agency officials.

As shown in table 3, five financial agency agreements accounted for 87 percent of the total obligated value through fiscal year 2011—about $476 million out of about $547 million. The vast majority of these obligations, approximately $383 million, went to Fannie Mae and Freddie Mac, which provide administrative and compliance services, respectively, for HAMP.[55]

---

[55]Congress established Fannie Mae and Freddie Mac as for-profit, shareholder-owned corporations to stabilize and assist the U.S. secondary mortgage market and facilitate the flow of mortgage credit.

GAO-12-229 Troubled Asset Relief Program

Table 3: Top Five Financial Agency Agreements

Financial agent (award date-completion date including options to extend agreement)	TARP investment program	Obligated value through fiscal year 2010	Obligated value through fiscal year 2011	Percent increase from fiscal year 2010
Fannie Mae (2/18/2009-2/17/2019)	HAMP	$126,712,000	$239,870,429	89%
Freddie Mac (2/18/2009-2/17/2019)	HAMP	88,850,000	143,060,025	61
Bank of New York Mellon (10/14/2008-10/14/2015)	All programs	28,495,411	42,108,749	48
AllianceBernstein (4/21/2009-4/20/2018)	• CPP • AIFP • AIG Investments	22,399,943	33,213,445	48
FSI Group (4/21/2009-4/20/2018)	• CPP • Asset Guarantee Program	11,102,500	18,041,838	63
Total		**$277,559,854**	**$476,294,486**	**72%**

Source: GAO analysis of Treasury data.

Treasury also heavily relies on contractors to help administer TARP programs. Treasury uses TARP contracts for a variety of legal, investment consulting, accounting, and other services and supplies. Through fiscal year 2011, Treasury had awarded or used 116 contracts and blanket purchase agreements, up from 81 last year, and about half of them remain active.[56] As shown in table 2, the total obligated value of these contracts has increased 42 percent since 2010, from $109 million to $155 million. About 75 percent of the contracts and blanket purchase agreements are relatively small (less than $1 million each). The two largest contracts are $33 million (with PricewaterhouseCoopers, LLP for internal control services) and $17 million (with Cadwalader, Wickersham & Taft, LLP for legal services).

From the outset, Treasury encouraged small and minority- and women-owned businesses to pursue opportunities for TARP contracts and financial agency agreements. The number of contracts and financial agency agreements that went to small and minority-owned businesses increased since 2010 from 16 to 31 (as shown in table 4). Also, 6 of the

[56]The 116 contracts and blanket purchase agreements include 6 contractual arrangements in which OFS is engaging vendors that have existing contracts with other Treasury offices or bureaus or with other federal agencies.

17 total financial agency agreements and 25 of the 116 total contracts were with these businesses through 2011. In addition, 73 subcontracts under financial agency agreements and prime contracts went to small and/or minority- and women-owned businesses. As in previous years, the majority of these businesses participating in TARP are subcontractors.

Table 4: TARP Contracts, Financial Agency Agreements, and Subcontracts with Small and Minority- and Women-Owned Businesses through Fiscal Years 2010 and 2011

	Fiscal year							
	2010	2011	2010	2011	2010	2011	2010	2011
Business category	Prime contracts[a]		Financial agency agreements[a]		Subcontracts under prime contracts and contracts under financial agency agreements[b]		Total participation by small businesses	
Minority-owned[c]	0	0	5	5	16	16	21	21
Woman-owned	2	5	1	1	14	20	17	26
Other small[d]	8	20	0	0	19	37	27	57
Total	**10**	**25**	**6**	**6**	**49**	**73**	**65**	**104**

Source: GAO analysis of Treasury data.

[a]Data as of September 30, 2011. GAO's analysis does not include task orders.

[b]As of September 30, 2011, TARP financial agents and prime contractors had awarded 130 subcontracts.

[c]Includes both small and nonsmall minority-owned businesses and minority woman-owned businesses.

[d]Includes small businesses, service-disabled veteran-owned small businesses, and small disadvantaged businesses.

Treasury Has Continued to Strengthen Management and Oversight of Financial Agents and Contractors and Conflicts-of-Interest Requirements

As we have reported, when Treasury began to quickly implement TARP initiatives in 2008, OFS had not finalized its procurement oversight procedures and lacked comprehensive internal controls for contractors and financial agents. Further, it did not have a comprehensive compliance system to monitor and fully address vendor-related conflicts of interest. Last year we reported that OFS had put in place an appropriate infrastructure to manage and monitor its network of financial agents and contractors. Specifically, by the end of fiscal year 2010, OFS had:

- defined organizational roles and responsibilities and established written policies and procedures for the management and oversight of TARP financial agents;

- taken action to ensure that sufficient personnel were assigned and properly trained to oversee the performance of financial agents and contractors;

- issued written procedures on measuring the performance of financial agents and installed qualitative and quantitative performance measures for several of its financial agents; and

- issued regulations on conflicts of interest, established an internal reporting system for tracking all vendor conflict-of-interest certifications, inquiries, and requests for waivers, and completed renegotiations of three contracts that predated the regulations.

In fiscal year 2011, Treasury continued to strengthen its policies and procedures for managing financial agents and contractors and conflicts of interest. For example, contract administration personnel made improvements to OFS's contract record system, including controls and clear deadlines for validating and certifying the completeness and accuracy of the information.[57] According to an OFS official responsible for contracting, contract administration personnel audited most of the items in the record system by tracing the items back to source documents, and found some areas that needed to be improved. Data fields that were used for informational purposes only, such as the contract specialist's telephone number, were not selected for audit. Fields selected included date of award, contractor, potential contract value, and socioeconomic status. Contract actions were matched against data in the Federal Procurement Data System-Next Generation before deciding whether the items needed to be traced back to source documents.[58] According to the official, new controls were established for adding new contract information to the system and documentation procedures were developed to improve data consistency.

The Office of Financial Agents (OFA) also expanded its implementation of performance assessments of financial agents by issuing performance

---

[57]OFS's contract record system is an Excel spreadsheet that contains the award date; performance end date; obligations to date; socioeconomic category; description of services; and other information related to its contracts, financial agency agreements, and interagency agreements.

[58]The Federal Procurement Data System-Next Generation is the federal government's primary data system for tracking information on contracting actions.

measures and initiating assessments for five additional financial agents, including Fannie Mae. Quarterly performance assessments are now conducted for all of the active financial agents. OFA establishes qualitative and quantitative performance measures, with input from the financial agent, based on the core functions and responsibilities described in each financial agency agreement. OFA staff review financial agents' performance against the qualitative and quantitative measures and prepare an overall performance assessment. The OFA reviews have identified areas in which a financial agent is performing above expectations or needs improvement. According to an OFA official, the performance reviews have been an important management tool and helped improve compliance through active communication and dialog with the financial agents. For those financial agents eligible to receive incentive payments, the performance reviews can affect the amount of payment.[59] OFA may revise the performance measures annually to ensure continued alignment with the financial agents' scope of work and OFS priorities.

The OIR took several actions to strengthen oversight of conflicts-of-interest requirements over the last year. Specifically, we found the following:

- OIR began conducting on-site compliance reviews to determine whether financial agents' internal controls and procedures are working. According to Treasury officials, six reviews were conducted in fiscal year 2011. Treasury found that five of the financial agents reviewed had reasonable internal controls in place. There were no significant findings, although OIR made some recommendations. The review of the remaining financial agent identified significant weaknesses in its controls and in organizational management and oversight. As a result of the review, the relationship with the financial agent was terminated. Thus far, the on-site compliance reviews have been of financial agents, but OIR plans to begin reviewing contractors in the near future.

---

[59]According to Treasury officials, incentive payments for exceeding performance measures are not available for Freddie Mac, Fannie Mae, Lazard Frères, EARNEST Partners, Morgan Stanley, Greenhill and Co., and Perella Weinberg Partners based on the terms of the agreements.

- In 2011, OIR began preparing a quarterly conflicts-of-interest feedback report for contractors. The report is shared with the Contracting Officer's Technical Representatives and included in the contractor performance metrics that are incorporated into Contract and Agreement Review Board reports.[60] OIR's reports describe and rate contractors' performance during the quarter in identifying, mitigating, and disclosing conflicts of interest to the Treasury; submitting adequate conflicts-of-interest certifications in a timely manner; and expeditiously responding to requests for additional information, among other things.

- In 2011, according to OFS's Compliance Officer, OIR put in place a requirement that all new contractors and financial agents, as well as Contracting Officer's Technical Representatives and OFA personnel with similar responsibilities, receive conflict-of-interest training. The training materials used are similar to those used before 2011, but the information presented is more consistent across all the training materials than it was before the formalization of the requirement.

- OIR continued to review a large number of inquiries from financial agents and contractors about potential conflicts of interest. The total reviewed as of September 30, 2011, was about 1,300, compared to about 655 through fiscal year 2010. Reasons given by OIR for the increase in inquiries in fiscal year 2011 compared with prior fiscal years include the addition of several new contractors and financial agents in fiscal year 2011 and the initiation of new processes, such as on-site reviews of entities' conflicts-of-interest controls. Forty-five of the 1,300 inquiries have resulted in waivers, including 8 waivers during fiscal year 2011. According to OFS's Compliance Officer, examples of waivers include permitting contractors and financial agents to utilize Office of Government Ethics Form 450 in place of the Form 278 and allowing contractors and financial agents to use their own entertainment and gift policies in place of those in Treasury's

---

[60]OFS's Contract and Agreement Review Board, which is composed of program and procurement executives, oversees OFS's acquisition decisions. The Board centralizes decisions regarding the office's contracting and financial agency requirements, serving as the deliberative body for determining whether to perform a function in house or to outsource it. This formalized process was established in March 2009, after the urgency of the initial stages of the financial crisis had subsided. Contracting Officer's Technical Representatives perform critical acquisition and technical functions, and contracting officers rely on them to ensure that contracts are managed properly to meet mission needs.

conflicts-of-interest regulation. OIR has never waived an actual or potential conflict of interest.

Staffing related to management and oversight of financial agents, contractors, and conflicts of interest has remained stable. However, a temporary loss of contract administration positions occurred when the Procurement Services Division transitioned to the Internal Revenue Service (IRS) in fiscal year 2011 as part of a Treasury-wide consolidation to improve departmental offices' procurement.[61] Treasury hopes to realize cost savings from the consolidation, improve internal controls and risk management, and enhance employee career development. According to an OFS contract administration official, several procurement positions were lost in the transition to IRS because staff did not want to move to the IRS facility in Oxon Hill, Maryland. IRS has agreed to staff a dedicated team of ten individuals to support OFS, the same level as before the move, and the team is currently being staffed by three federal employees and two contractors, with plans to expand to six federal employees and four contractors. According to the official, the procurement work is a partnership between OFS and IRS, with OFS identifying vendors in conjunction with IRS, IRS awarding the contracts, and OFS and IRS sharing post-award duties, such as managing vendors, invoicing, and keeping records.[62]

---

[61]The former Procurement Services Division supported Treasury Departmental Offices (DO) procurement, including domestic finance, economic policy, and general counsel, and OFS was one of its customers. According to a Treasury acquisition procedures update in August 2011, the IRS Procurement Office now supports DO as a result of transition of the DO Procurement Services Division to the IRS Procurement Office. According to the update, effective and efficient use of Treasury's procurement resources is imperative to responsible execution of the department's procurement authority.

[62]In addition to OFS's staffing, contracting, and financial agent agreement management, we have also reviewed other elements of Treasury's implementation of TARP. Since 2009, we have audited and issued an opinion on OFS's financial statements and its internal control over financial reporting. Our most recent financial statement audit concluded that although certain internal controls could be improved, OFS maintained in all material respects effective internal control over financial reporting as of September 30, 2011, that provided reasonable assurance that misstatements, losses, or noncompliance material in relation to the financial statements would be prevented or detected and corrected in a timely manner. See GAO-12-169.

Although Estimated Lifetime TARP Costs Have Decreased Significantly, Treasury Could Enhance Its Communication about the Costs of TARP

While lifetime cost estimates for TARP have decreased since the government first provided assistance in 2008, the lifetime cost and income estimates for specific TARP programs have fluctuated with changes in program activity and the market value of Treasury's TARP investments. Although Treasury issues several reports on the costs of TARP, its communications about TARP costs in press releases is inconsistent and could be enhanced. Moreover, indirect costs such as moral hazard are also associated with TARP and remain a concern.

Estimated Direct TARP Costs Have Decreased Significantly

As of September 30, 2011, Treasury has incurred net costs of $28 billion, while recent federal lifetime cost projections for TARP—which include both realized and future cash flows—have decreased. In 2009, the Congressional Budget Office (CBO) estimated that TARP could cost $356 billion.[63] However, CBO's most recent estimate, using November 2011 data, is approximately $34 billion.[64] Treasury's fiscal year 2011 financial statement, audited by GAO, reported that TARP would cost around $70 billion as of September 30, 2011, a decrease from about $78 billion estimated as of September 2010. In general, the variation in CBO and Treasury cost estimates is attributable to their timing—that is, market conditions and program activities differed when the estimates were developed. However, program participation assumptions for TARP-funded housing programs explain the large difference between the CBO and Treasury cost estimates. Treasury assumed that all of the $45.6 billion allocated to TARP housing programs would be utilized and, as a result, estimated that they would cost $45.6 billion. Conversely, CBO expected lower participation rates for the housing programs, resulting in a cost estimate of $13 billion as of November 2011. While these differences exist, CBO officials noted that as TARP continues to wind down, Treasury's and CBO's lifetime cost estimates should be more similar. This convergence of cost estimates is likely to occur as program costs become clearer and more recipients repay their assistance—reducing the number

---

[63]For more information on the cost estimate calculation, see Congressional Budget Office, *The Troubled Asset Relief Program: Report on Transactions through June 17, 2009* (Washington, D.C.: June 2009).

[64]For CBO's recent cost estimate, see Congressional Budget Office, *Report on the Troubled Asset Relief Program—December 2011* (Washington, D.C.: Dec. 16, 2011).

of outstanding TARP assets and the related uncertainty about how market risks will affect the future value of these investments.

In our review of Treasury's lifetime cost estimates for TARP's equity investment programs, we found that the estimates for some programs changed only slightly, if at all, between September 2010 and September 2011, while others changed by a notable margin. For example, Treasury estimated that CPP would result in lifetime income of $11.2 billion as of September 2010 and its recent estimate as of September 2011 was slightly higher at $13 billion (see fig. 15). This increase in CPP's estimated lifetime income was the result of proceeds in excess of costs from the sale of Citigroup common stock offset by a decline in the estimated market value of Treasury's remaining CPP investments. Additionally, Treasury's lifetime cost estimate of $45.6 billion for TARP-funded housing programs remained unchanged between September 2010 and September 2011 because Treasury continues to assume that all of the $45.6 billion allocated to the housing programs will be utilized.

On the other hand, Treasury's recent cost estimates for AIFP and assistance to AIG changed markedly when compared to estimates as of September 2010. Specifically, Treasury estimated a lifetime cost of $14.7 billion for AIFP as of September 2010 but that estimate increased to $23.6 billion using September 2011 data due to a decline in the value of Treasury's equity investments in GM and Ally Financial. Additionally, Treasury's estimate for assistance to AIG decreased from $36.9 billion to $24.3 billion between September 2010 and September 2011 as a result of improvements in the financial condition of AIG since Treasury first provided assistance and the restructuring of Treasury's AIG investment to common stock. However, as we have seen, the ultimate cost of the assistance to AIG could be about $11.5 billion after factoring in the estimated lifetime income of $12.8 billion from Treasury's non-TARP assistance to AIG.[65] As shown, lifetime cost estimates are likely to fluctuate, particularly for investment programs like AIFP and the AIG Investment Program, because future results rely heavily on the market price of common stock.

---

[65]Treasury estimates lifetime income of approximately $12.8 billion from the sale of its non-TARP AIG shares which could offset the estimated lifetime cost of $24.3 billion associated with its TARP shares in AIG. See figure 8 in the AIG section for more details.

GAO-12-229 Troubled Asset Relief Program

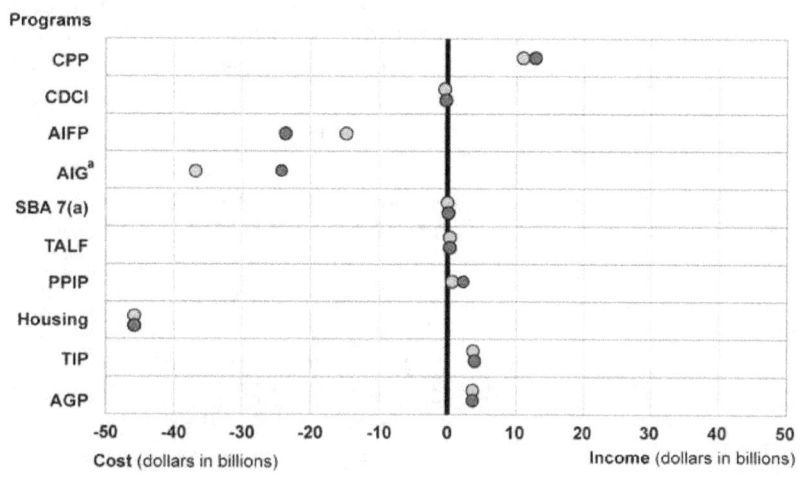

Figure 15: Comparison of Treasury's Lifetime Cost and Income Estimates for TARP Programs, September 30, 2010, and September 30, 2011

○ September 30, 2010 estimate
● September 30, 2011 estimate

Source: GAO analysis of Treasury data.

[a]Although Treasury's cost estimate for its AIG TARP common stock is $24.3 billion, the overall cost of AIG, including the income expected from the AIG non-TARP common stock, could be approximately $11.5 billion based on recent cost estimates (see AIG-related discussion earlier in this report).

Treasury's Press Releases Inconsistently Include Cost Information

Although Treasury regularly reports on the cost of TARP and its programs, it could improve the clarity and consistency of its communications on TARP costs, specifically in its press releases about specific programs. Treasury issues several reports—including the Agency Financial Report, Monthly 105(a) Reports, and Transaction Reports—that provide updates on the funds obligated and disbursed, repayments and income, and gains and losses. Compared to Treasury's past reporting practices, recent versions of the Agency Financial Report and the Monthly 105(a) Reports clearly present Treasury's lifetime cost estimates for TARP and its programs.[66] However, Treasury's press releases do not

---

[66]For examples of Treasury's lifetime subsidy cost estimates for TARP programs see Department of the Treasury, Office of Financial Stability, *Troubled Asset Relief Program Agency Financial Report Fiscal Year 2010* (Washington, D.C.: 2010), and Department of the Treasury, *Troubled Asset Relief Program Monthly 105(a) Report—December 2010* (Washington, D.C.: Jan. 10, 2011).

consistently include these cost estimates. Rather, Treasury's press releases on specific TARP programs typically only include transaction-oriented updates, such as disbursements and returns on Treasury's investments from repayments, dividends, and the sale of its assets. While the transaction-oriented updates in Treasury's press releases are important, they do not provide the general public with the greater context—the lifetime cost associated with individual programs.[67]

Furthermore, it appears that over the last 2 years Treasury has included lifetime cost estimates in some of its program-specific press releases for programs expected to result in a lifetime income, while excluding these estimates for programs expected to result in a cost for taxpayers. For instance, a press release from April 2011 indicated that Treasury's bank programs were expected to result in a lifetime positive return of approximately $20 billion. Other press releases for TARP banking programs also include this reference to expected lifetime income. However, during the same period Treasury did not include lifetime cost estimates in its press releases for TARP programs that projected a cost to the government, such as SBA 7(a), AIG, and AIFP. For example, Treasury issued a press release in June 2011 that described its sale of several SBA 7(a) securities. Treasury stated that the sale resulted in overall gains and income. The content of this press release implied that the program had earned a significant amount of money but did not provide the more comprehensive lifetime cost estimate for the program, which was $1 million at that time. In addition, over the last 2 years none of Treasury's press releases for AIG and AIFP (programs expected to cost approximately $24.3 billion and $23.6 billion respectively, as of September 30, 2011) have included the lifetime cost estimates associated with the programs.[68] Rather, they have generally discussed Treasury's investment in the programs and revenues received. This inconsistent disclosure of lifetime cost estimates raises concerns about the consistency and transparency of Treasury's press releases and suggests a selective approach that focuses on reporting program lifetime income and not lifetime costs.

---

[67] For additional information on the lifetime cost calculation required by the Federal Credit Reform Act of 1990 see Treasury, *Troubled Asset Relief Program Agency Financial Report Fiscal Year 2010*.

[68] As noted earlier in this report, the $24.3 billion is associated with TARP-related assistance. Factoring in income of $12.8 billion for its non-TARP shares could result in a net estimated cost of $11.5 billion.

As we have previously reported, transparency is important in the context of TARP and the unprecedented government assistance it provided to the financial sector. In discussing our questions about the press releases with Treasury officials, they noted that they provide cost information in other public reports. However, by improving the clarity of its communication on the costs of TARP through consistently incorporating lifetime cost estimates into its program press releases, Treasury could reduce potential confusion and misunderstanding of TARP's results. Treasury would also be setting a precedent for cost reporting associated with any future government interventions.

Despite Estimated Decreases in TARP Costs, Government Interventions Such as TARP Can Exacerbate Moral Hazard

Though direct costs for TARP—including potential lifetime income—can be estimated and quantified, certain indirect costs connected to the government's assistance are less easily measured. For example, as we have previously reported, when the government provides assistance to the private sector, it may increase moral hazard that would then need to be mitigated.[69] That is, in the face of government assistance, private firms are motivated to take risks they might not take in the absence of such assistance, or creditors may not price into their extensions of credit the full risk assumed by the firm, believing that the government would provide assistance should the firm become distressed.

EESA and the amendments made by the American Recovery and Reinvestment Act of 2009 established a number of measures to mitigate the moral hazard of TARP by requiring that participating institutions follow certain requirements. These include providing Treasury with warrants in exchange for TARP funds to allow taxpayers to benefit from any appreciation of the company's stock, and limiting certain bonuses and golden parachute payments for certain highly compensated employees and senior executive officers, as such payments can encourage excessive risk-taking. Even with such requirements in place, however, government intervention in the private sector can encourage market participants to expect similar emergency actions. This belief diminishes market discipline as it can weaken private or market-based incentives to

---

[69]See GAO, *Financial Assistance: Ongoing Challenges and Guiding Principles Related to Government Assistance For Private Sector Companies,* GAO-10-719 (Washington, D.C.: Aug. 3, 2010).

properly manage risks and can in particular contribute to the perception that some firms are "too big to fail."[70]

Government interventions can also have consequences for the banking industry as a whole, including institutions that do not receive bailout funds. For instance, investors may perceive the debt associated with institutions that received government assistance as being less risky because of the potential for future government bailouts. This perception could lead them to choose to invest in such assisted institutions instead of those that did not receive assistance. However, such effects may be temporary, as evidenced by the recent downgrade by Moody's Investors Service, Inc. (Moody's) of the long-term credit ratings of Bank of America Corp. and Wells Fargo & Co. after the Dodd-Frank Act's new regulatory provisions were enacted into law, which aim to avoid or at least limit future government bailouts to financial institutions. Moody's stated that it downgraded these credit ratings because it believes the government is less likely to rescue these financial institutions now than it was during the financial crisis. This rating change could affect their ability to access financing with as favorable terms.

The Dodd-Frank Act included a number of provisions intended to address the problem of "too big to fail" by strengthening oversight of financial institutions. For example, the Dodd-Frank Act required the Federal Reserve to implement enhanced prudential standards for bank holding companies that are deemed systemically important and increased oversight of certain nonbank financial companies. Specifically, the Federal Reserve has been given supervisory authority over any nonbank financial company that the Financial Stability Oversight Council

---

[70]The term "too big too fail" can also include "too interconnected to fail" and other terms that signify that a failure of a particular institution would have a significant negative effect on the broader financial system or economy.

determines could pose a threat to the financial stability of the country.[71] Also, the Dodd-Frank Act provided new reporting and resolution authorities to the Federal Deposit Insurance Corporation for certain large, systemic financial institutions, and requires those institutions to write plans for their unwinding.[72] However, if these new provisions fail to address the too big to fail phenomenon, future financial crises could emerge that may be similar or worse than the financial meltdown that escalated with the failures of Bear Stearns and Lehman Brothers in 2008. That is, some firms may see the government assistance that was provided during the last crisis as a promise of similar aid in the future and therefore have an incentive to continue engaging in risky activities. Ultimately, any moral hazard effects of the Dodd-Frank Act changes will not be known until financial institutions face another period of financial stress.

Conclusions

As Treasury continues to unwind most TARP programs, the estimated costs of TARP have decreased significantly from when Treasury first announced TARP. Treasury's latest estimate of approximately $70 billion as of September 30, 2011, includes a large projection of lifetime income from CPP, and the cost estimates for assistance to AIG and the auto

---

[71]The purpose of the Financial Stability Oversight Council is to (1) identify risks to the financial stability of the U.S. from the financial distress, failure, or activities of large interconnected bank holding companies or nonbank financial companies; (2) promote market discipline by eliminating expectations that the government will shield shareholders, creditors, and other counterparties from losses in the event of failure; and (3) respond to emerging threats to the stability of the U.S. financial system. The Council is made up of the following voting members: the Secretary of the Treasury, the Chairman of the Federal Reserve, the Comptroller of the Currency, the Director of the Bureau of Consumer Financial Protection, the Chairman of the Securities and Exchange Commission, the Chairperson of the Federal Deposit Insurance Corporation, the Chairperson of the Commodity Futures Trading Commission, the Director of the Federal Housing Finance Agency, the Chairman of the National Credit Union Administration Board, and an independent member appointed by the President who is approved by the Senate and has insurance expertise. The Council's nonvoting members include the Director of the Office of Financial Research, the Director of the Federal Insurance Office, a state insurance commissioner, state securities commissioner, and state banking supervisor.

[72]On November 1, 2011, the Federal Deposit Insurance Corporation and the Federal Reserve published in the Federal Register a final rule implementing the resolution plan requirements for large bank holding companies and nonbank financial companies supervised by the Federal Reserve. The final rule is effective November 30, 2011. The Federal Deposit Insurance Corporation also issued a complementary interim final rule, published in September 2011 that is effective in January 2012.

GAO-12-229 Troubled Asset Relief Program

companies continue to fluctuate, demonstrating that such estimates are subject to price movements in the market, among other factors, and could change in the future. We found that Treasury enhanced some of its cost reporting in the past year, although its press releases require improvements. Such communications about specific programs include information about estimated lifetime costs and income only when programs are expected to result in lifetime income and not when they are expected to result in a lifetime cost. This practice does not represent a consistent approach to reporting to the public through press releases on the costs of individual programs. As we have indicated in many past reports on TARP, transparency remains a critical element to the government's unprecedented assistance to the financial sector. Such transparency helps clarify to the public the costs of TARP assistance and to understand how the government intervened in various markets. Enhancing the transparency and clarity of these press releases will also set a precedent for any future government interventions, should they ever be needed.

Recommendation for Executive Action

To enhance transparency about the costs of TARP programs as Treasury unwinds its involvement, we recommend that the Secretary of the Treasury enhance Treasury's communications with the public, in particular Treasury's press releases, about TARP programs and costs by consistently including information on estimated lifetime costs, especially when reporting on program results. For example, Treasury should consider including lifetime cost estimates, or references to Treasury reports that include such information, in its press releases about specific programs.

Agency Comments and Our Evaluation

We provided a draft of this report to Treasury for its review and comment. Treasury provided written comments that we have reprinted in appendix III. Treasury also provided technical comments that we have incorporated as appropriate.

In its written comments, Treasury agreed with our recommendation that it could further enhance its communications about the costs of TARP programs in its program-specific press releases, also noting that it has established comprehensive accountability and transparency regarding TARP. Treasury stated that it will implement our recommendation by including a link to its Monthly 105(a) Report, which contains cost estimates for each TARP program, in its future program-specific press releases. Implementation of our recommendation through this practice would provide a good opportunity for Treasury to clearly and fully communicate TARP program costs to the public.

We are sending copies of this report to the Financial Stability Oversight Board, Special Inspector General for TARP, interested congressional committees and members, and Treasury. The report also is available at no charge on the GAO website at http://www.gao.gov.

If you or your staffs have any questions about this report, please contact Orice Williams Brown at (202) 512-8678 or williamso@gao.gov, A. Nicole Clowers at (202) 512-8678 or clowersa@gao.gov, or Thomas J. McCool at (202) 512-2642 or mccoolt@gao.gov. Contact points for our Offices of Congressional Relations and Public Affairs may be found on the last page of this report. GAO staff who made major contributions to this report are listed in appendix IV.

Thomas J. McCool

Thomas J. McCool
Director
Center for Economics, Applied Research and Methods

List of Addressees

The Honorable Daniel K. Inouye
Chairman
The Honorable Thad Cochran
Vice Chairman
Committee on Appropriations
United States Senate

The Honorable Tim Johnson
Chairman
The Honorable Richard C. Shelby
Ranking Member
Committee on Banking, Housing, and Urban Affairs
United States Senate

The Honorable Kent Conrad
Chairman
The Honorable Jeff Sessions
Ranking Member
Committee on the Budget
United States Senate

The Honorable Max Baucus
Chairman
The Honorable Orrin G. Hatch
Ranking Member
Committee on Finance
United States Senate

The Honorable Hal Rogers
Chairman
The Honorable Norm Dicks
Ranking Member
Committee on Appropriations
House of Representatives

The Honorable Paul Ryan
Chairman
The Honorable Chris Van Hollen
Ranking Member
Committee on the Budget
House of Representatives

The Honorable Spencer Bachus
Chairman
The Honorable Barney Frank
Ranking Member
Committee on Financial Services
House of Representatives

The Honorable Dave Camp
Chairman
The Honorable Sandy Levin
Ranking Member
Committee on Ways and Means
House of Representative

Appendix I: Scope and Methodology

To assess the condition and status of all programs initiated under the Troubled Asset Relief Program (TARP), we collected and analyzed data about program utilization and assets held, as applicable, focusing primarily on financial information that we had audited in the Office of Financial Stability's (OFS) financial statements, as of September 30, 2011. As noted in the report, in some instances we provided more recent, unaudited financial information. The financial information includes the types of assets held in the program, obligations that represent the highest amount ever obligated for a program (to provide historical information on total obligations), disbursements, and income. We also provide information on program start dates, defining them based on the start of the first activity under a program, and we provide program end dates, based on official announcements or program terms from the Department of the Treasury (Treasury). Finally, we provide approximate program exit dates—either estimated by Treasury or actual if the exit already occurred—that reflect the time when a program will no longer hold assets that need to be managed. We also used OFS cost estimates for TARP that we audited as part of the financial statement audit and reviewed Congressional Budget Office (CBO) cost estimates from publicly available CBO reports. In addition, we tested OFS's internal controls over financial reporting as it relates to our annual audit of OFS's financial statements. The financial information used in this report is sufficiently reliable to assess the condition and status of TARP programs based on the results of our audits of fiscal years 2009, 2010, and 2011 financial statements for TARP.[1]

We also examined Treasury documentation such as program terms, decision memos, press releases, and reports on TARP programs and costs. Also, we interviewed OFS program officials to determine the current status of each TARP program, the role of TARP staff while most programs continue to unwind, and to update what is known about exit considerations for TARP programs. Other TARP officials we interviewed included those responsible for financial reporting. Additionally, in reporting on these programs and their exit considerations we leveraged our previous TARP reports and publications from the Special Inspector General for TARP and the Congressional Oversight Panel, as appropriate. In addition:

---

[1]See GAO-12-169, GAO-11-174, and GAO-10-301.

- For the Capital Purchase Program, we used OFS' reports to describe the status of the program, including amount of investments outstanding, the number of institutions that had repaid their investments, and the amount of dividends paid, among other things. In addition, we reviewed Treasury's press releases on the program. We also relied on information that we have collected as part of our ongoing review of the financial condition of Capital Purchase Program institutions.

- For the Community Development Capital Initiative, we interviewed program officials to determine how the program is managed and what repayment or exit concerns Treasury has for the program.

- To update the status of the Automotive Industry Financing Program (AIFP) and Treasury's plans for managing its investment in the companies, we leveraged our past work; reviewed information on Treasury's exit from Chrysler, including Chrysler and Treasury press releases; reviewed information on Treasury's plans for overseeing its remaining financial interests in General Motors (GM) and Ally Financial, including Administration and Treasury reports. To obtain information on the current financial condition of the companies, we reviewed information on GM's and Ally Financial's finances and operations, including financial statements and industry analysts' reports.

- To update the status of the American International Group, Inc. (AIG) Investment Program (formerly the Systemically Significant Failing Institutions Program) we reviewed relevant documents from Treasury and other parties. For the AIG Investment Program, these documents included 105(a) reports provided periodically to Congress by Treasury, as well as reports produced by the Board of Governors of the Federal Reserve System, and the Federal Reserve Bank of New York, and other relevant documentation such as AIG's financial disclosures and Treasury's press releases. We also interviewed officials from each of these agencies and AIG.

- For the Small Business Administration (SBA) 7(a) Securities Purchase Program, we analyzed data on Treasury purchases and dispositions of SBA 7(a) securities collected during our financial audit. We also reviewed decision memos on the disposition of the SBA 7(a) portfolio. In addition, we reviewed press releases about the program's sales activity and income. We reviewed SBA 7(a) loan volume data provided by Treasury and compared that to trends in our past reports related to SBA 7(a) lending and we also interviewed program staff about the status of the programs and plans for future sales.

- For the Term Asset-Backed Securities Loan Facility (TALF), we reviewed program terms and requested data from Treasury about loan prepayments and TALF LLC activity. We also researched trends in the values of commercial mortgage-backed securities. Additionally, we interviewed OFS officials about their role in the program as it continues to unwind.

- To update the status of the Public-Private Investment Program, we analyzed program quarterly reports, term sheets, and other documentation related to the public-private investment funds. We also interviewed OFS staff responsible for the program to determine the status of the program while it remains in active investment status.

- To determine the status of Treasury's TARP-funded housing programs, we obtained and reviewed Treasury's published reports on the programs and servicer performance, documentation on projected cost estimates and disbursements for each of the programs, and guidelines and related updates issued by Treasury for each of the programs. In addition, we obtained information from and interviewed Treasury officials about the status of the TARP-funded housing programs, including numbers of borrowers helped and the actions Treasury had taken to address our prior recommendations.

- To obtain the final status for three programs that Treasury exited and for which Treasury no longer holds assets that it must manage—the Asset Guarantee Program, Capital Assistance Program, and Targeted Investment Program—we reviewed Treasury's recent reports and leveraged our past work.

To determine the proportion of permanent, term, and detailee staff in OFS, we reviewed program data showing changes in the number of staff over time and in each OFS office. We assessed this staffing data for reliability by comparing it to organizational directories to ensure that the changes were generally equivalent. We determined that the staffing data was sufficiently reliable to show trends in OFS staffing. We also interviewed agency officials to gain insight into the trends. Additionally, we obtained program-specific staffing information from agency officials during interviews to inform our discussion of the staffing needs of each TARP program and any succession planning undertaken by OFS. Also, we reviewed OFS documentation, such as the organizational directories, to analyze any changes in leadership positions in OFS. To assess the staffing challenges of OFS as TARP continues to wind down, we reviewed past GAO reports and recommendations and the OFS staffing and development plan, and we interviewed agency officials.

To assess OFS's use of financial agents and contractors since TARP was established in October 2008, we reviewed information on financial agents and contractors from OFS's contract record system and interviewed Treasury contract officials about financial agency agreements, contracts, and blanket purchase agreements as of September 30, 2011, that support TARP administration and programs. We analyzed information from the contract record system to update key details on the status of TARP financial agents and contractors, such as total number of agreements and contracts, type of services being performed, obligated values, periods of performance, and share of work by small businesses. Through discussions with Treasury officials responsible for the contract record system and inquiries we made about selected data items, as well as matching OFS's contract list against data we obtained from the Federal Procurement Data System-Next Generation, we determined that data in the record system were sufficiently reliable for our purposes. To assess OFS's progress in strengthening its infrastructure for managing and overseeing the performance of TARP financial agents and contractors and addressing conflicts of interest that could arise with the use of private sector firms, we reviewed various documents and interviewed OFS officials about changes in fiscal year 2011 to its policies and procedures regarding (1) management and oversight of TARP financial agents and contractors and (2) monitoring and oversight activities by the OFS team responsible for financial agent and contractor compliance with TARP conflicts-of-interest requirements. We did not review financial agents' performance assessments or incentive payments.

To ascertain what is known about TARP costs, we reviewed the cost reporting of CBO, the Office of Management and Budget (OMB), and Treasury, including the credit reform accounting methods used to develop cost estimates for TARP programs. For our analysis we focused on Treasury's cost estimates for the following reasons: (1) Treasury's recent financial statements and cost projections have been audited by GAO and (2) estimates reported by OMB are based on numbers provided by

Treasury.[2] We interviewed officials from CBO and Treasury on the methods used to calculate TARP costs and the reasons for any significant differences among the cost estimates calculated by each agency. We utilized data from our financial audit and leveraged other internal resources related to credit reform accounting and the modeling of TARP costs. We also reviewed Treasury's press releases on the costs of TARP. For our review of the moral hazards of TARP, we reviewed pertinent legislation such as the Emergency Economic Stabilization Act and the Dodd-Frank Wall Street Reform and Consumer Protection Act and utilized previous GAO reports and Congressional Oversight Panel publications.

We conducted this performance audit from June 2011 to January 2012 in accordance with generally accepted government auditing standards. Those standards require that we plan and perform the audit to obtain sufficient, appropriate evidence to provide a reasonable basis for our findings and conclusions based on our audit objectives. We believe that the evidence obtained provides a reasonable basis for our findings and conclusions based on our audit objectives.

---

[2]Although Treasury provides OMB with TARP transaction and cost estimate data, OMB may include different estimates in its reports than those reported by Treasury. For instance, Treasury typically reports lifetime cost estimates for TARP programs that include the interest on re-estimates whereas OMB often reports program lifetime cost estimates that do not include the interest on re-estimates. For more details about the interest on re-estimates, see Office of Management and Budget, *Circular No. A-11, Part 5, Section 185 Federal Credit* (Washington, D.C.: June 2008).

Appendix II: Information on Programs Treasury Has Exited

This appendix includes information about TARP programs that Treasury has exited and for which Treasury no longer holds assets to manage. We provide an overview of the purpose of these programs, when they started and ended, the status of funding, and the final lifetime costs or income of the programs, as applicable.

Asset Guarantee Program

The Asset Guarantee Program was established as the Treasury insurance program, which provided federal government assurances for assets held by financial institutions that were deemed critical to the functioning of the U.S. financial system. Citigroup and Bank of America were the only two institutions that participated in this program before it was terminated. As previously reported, Bank of America paid Treasury and others a fee for terminating the term sheet before any assets were segregated.[1] Treasury sold the remaining assets that it held related to this program in January 2011 with the sale of Citigroup warrants, though it could receive future monies from trust preferred stock held by the Federal Deposit Insurance Corporation. Treasury reports that lifetime income from terminating the Bank of America agreement and exiting Citigroup-related assets is $3.7 billion (see fig. 16).

---

[1]For additional details on the Asset Guarantee Program, Capital Assistance Program, and Targeted Investment Program, see GAO-11-74 and GAO-10-16.

Figure 16: Status of the Asset Guarantee Program, as of September 30, 2011

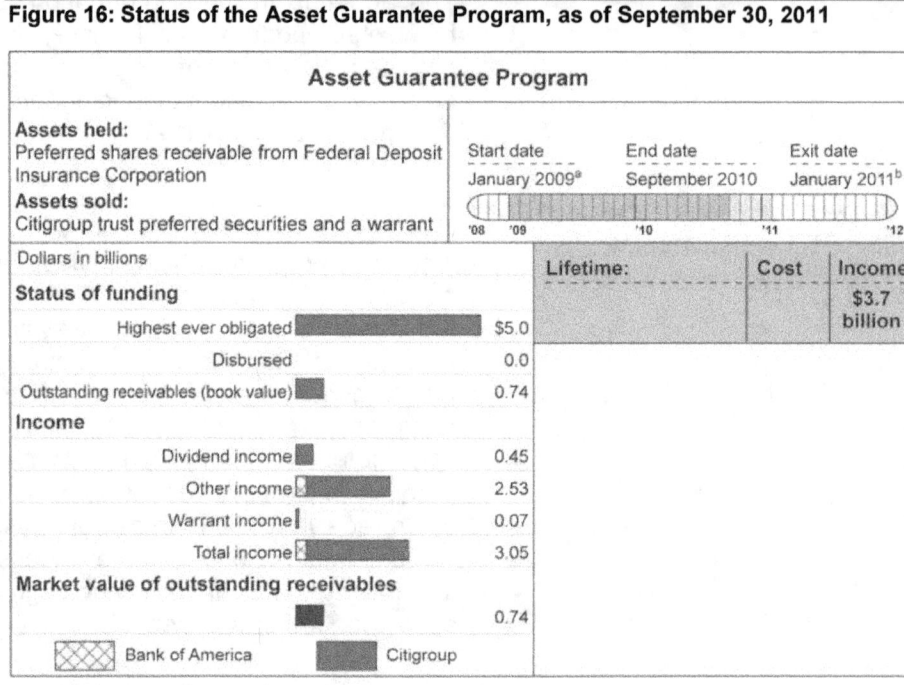

Source: GAO analysis of Treasury data.

[a]Treasury first announced assistance under this program in November 2008.

[b]Treasury no longer holds assets for this program that it needs to manage, though the Federal Deposit Insurance Corporation still holds Citigroup trust preferred stock and Treasury could receive income when these assets are sold.

Targeted Investment Program

The Targeted Investment Program was designed to foster market stability and thereby strengthen the economy by investing in institutions on a case-by-case basis that Treasury deemed critical to the functioning of the financial system. Only two institutions—Bank of America and Citigroup—participated in this program, and each received $20 billion in capital investment, which both repaid in December 2009. Treasury auctioned the Bank of America warrant that it received under the Targeted Investment Program in March 2010. Treasury auctioned the Citigroup warrant in January 2011. Treasury reports that lifetime income for this program totals $4 billion (see fig. 17).

Figure 17: Status of the Targeted Investment Program, as of September 30, 2011

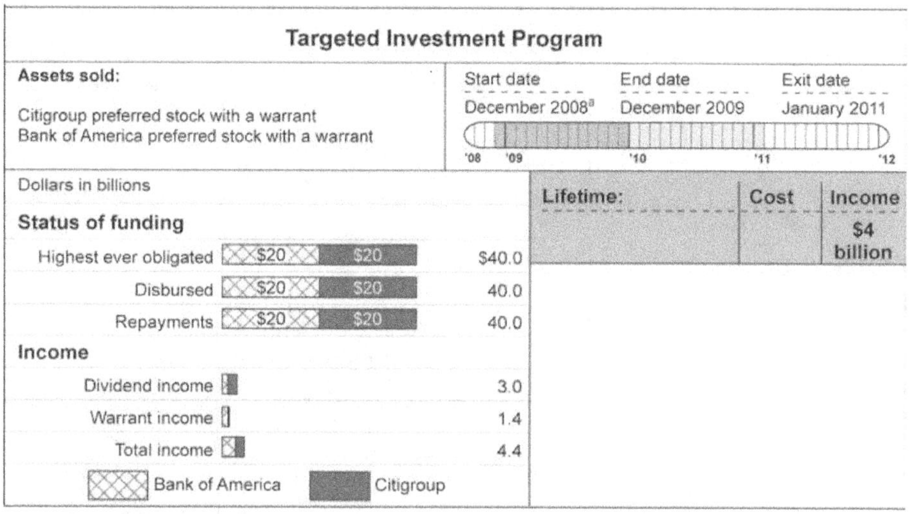

Targeted Investment Program

Assets sold:

Citigroup preferred stock with a warrant
Bank of America preferred stock with a warrant

	Start date	End date	Exit date
	December 2008[a]	December 2009	January 2011

'08 '09   '10   '11   '12

Dollars in billions

Status of funding

		Lifetime:	Cost	Income
Highest ever obligated	$20 $20 $40.0			$4 billion
Disbursed	$20 $20 40.0			
Repayments	$20 $20 40.0			

Income

Dividend income 3.0
Warrant income 1.4
Total income 4.4

⌧ Bank of America   ▮ Citigroup

Source: GAO analysis of Treasury data.

[a]Treasury first announced assistance under this program in November 2008.

Capital Assistance Program

The Capital Assistance Program was designed to further improve confidence in the banking system by helping ensure that the largest 19 U.S. bank holding companies had sufficient capital to cushion themselves against larger than expected future losses, as determined by the Supervisory Capital Assessment Program—or "stress test"—conducted by the federal banking regulators. The Capital Assistance Program was announced in February 2009 and ended in November 2009. It was never utilized.

Appendix III: Comments from the Department of the Treasury

DEPARTMENT OF THE TREASURY
WASHINGTON, D.C. 20220

ASSISTANT SECRETARY

December 14, 2011

Thomas J. McCool
Director, Center for Economics
Applied Research and Methods
U.S. Government Accountability Office
441 G Street, NW
Washington, DC 20548

Dear Mr. McCool:

I am writing in response to your draft report entitled, "*As Treasury Continues to Exit Programs, Opportunities to Enhance Communication on Costs Exist,*" provided to Treasury on November 23, 2011. The draft report provides a useful summary of the current condition and status of the Troubled Asset Relief Program (TARP); the Department of the Treasury's (Treasury) management of TARP operations; and the costs associated with TARP programs. This letter provides Treasury's official response to the GAO draft report.

Treasury appreciates GAO's recognition that "the estimated costs of TARP have decreased significantly from when Treasury first announced" the program. We agree. Indeed, TARP helped stop the widespread financial panic the nation faced in the fall of 2008, and did so at a fraction of the cost that most people expected when the law was passed. Likewise, we appreciate GAO's recognition that Treasury has appropriately addressed staffing levels and expertise in light of the temporary nature of TARP, and that Treasury "strengthen[ed] its policies and procedures for managing financial agents and contractors and conflicts of interest."

As you know, Treasury has established comprehensive accountability and transparency measures regarding TARP. Treasury publishes hundreds of reports and other information about TARP so that the public is made aware of how the money was spent, who received funds, and on what terms. We therefore appreciate GAO's acknowledgement that "the Agency Financial Report and the Monthly 105(a) reports clearly present Treasury's lifetime cost estimates for TARP and its programs." The draft report suggests that Treasury could further enhance transparency by consistently including lifetime cost estimates or references to reports containing such information in its program-specific press releases. We will implement this recommendation by including a link to our monthly 105(a) report -- which contains our most recent lifetime cost estimates -- in future TARP transaction press releases.

We appreciate the opportunity to respond to your draft report. Treasury values GAO's detailed
review of TARP and shares its underlying objective of continuously improving the program. We
look forward to continuing to work with you and your team as we move forward.

Sincerely,

Timothy G. Massad
Assistant Secretary for Financial Stability

Appendix IV: GAO Contacts and Staff Acknowledgments

GAO Contacts

Orice Williams Brown, (202) 512-8678 or williamso@gao.gov
A. Nicole Clowers, (202) 512-8678 or clowersa@gao.gov
Thomas J. McCool, (202) 512-2642 or mccoolt@gao.gov

Staff Acknowledgments

In addition to the contacts named above, Gary Engel, Mathew J. Scirè, and William T. Woods (lead Directors); Marcia Carlsen, Lawrance Evans, Jr., Dan Garcia-Diaz, Lynda Downing, Kay Kuhlman, Harry Medina, Joseph O'Neill, John Oppenheim, Raymond Sendejas, and Karen Tremba (lead Assistant Directors); Emily Chalmers; Rachel DeMarcus; John Forrester; Christopher Forys; Heather Krause; Robert Lee; Aaron Livernois; Dragan Matic; Emily Owens; Erin Schoening; and Mel Thomas have made significant contributions to this report.

Related GAO Products

Financial Audit: Office of Financial Stability (Troubled Asset Relief Program) Fiscal Years 2011 and 2010 Financial Statements. GAO-12-169. Washington, D.C.: November 10, 2011.

Troubled Asset Relief Program: Status of GAO Recommendations to Treasury. GAO-11-906R. Washington, D.C.: September 16, 2011.

Troubled Asset Relief Program: The Government's Exposure to AIG Following the Company's Recapitalization. GAO-11-716. Washington, D.C.: July 28, 2011.

Troubled Asset Relief Program: Results of Housing Counselors Survey on Borrowers' Experiences with the Home Affordable Modification Program. GAO-11-367R. Washington, D.C.: May 26, 2011.

Troubled Asset Relief Program: Survey of Housing Counselors about the Home Affordable Modification Program, an E-supplement to GAO-11-367R. GAO-11-368SP. Washington, D.C.: May 26, 2011.

TARP: Treasury's Exit from GM and Chrysler Highlights Competing Goals, and Results of Support to Auto Communities Are Unclear. GAO-11-471. Washington, D.C.: May 10, 2011.

Management Report: Improvements Are Needed in Internal Control Over Financial Reporting for the Troubled Asset Relief Program. GAO-11-434R. Washington, D.C.: April 18, 2011.

Troubled Asset Relief Program: Status of Programs and Implementation of GAO Recommendations. GAO-11-476T. Washington, D.C.: March 17, 2011.

Troubled Asset Relief Program: Treasury Continues to Face Implementation Challenges and Data Weaknesses in Its Making Home Affordable Program. GAO-11-288. Washington, D.C.: March 17, 2011.

Troubled Asset Relief Program: Actions Needed by Treasury to Address Challenges in Implementing Making Home Affordable Programs. GAO-11-338T. Washington, D.C.: March 2, 2011.

Troubled Asset Relief Program: Third Quarter 2010 Update of Government Assistance Provided to AIG and Description of Recent Execution of Recapitalization Plan. GAO-11-46. Washington, D.C.: January 20, 2011.

Troubled Asset Relief Program: Status of Programs and Implementation of GAO Recommendations. GAO-11-74. Washington, D.C.: January 12, 2011.

Financial Audit: Office of Financial Stability (Troubled Asset Relief Program) Fiscal Years 2010 and 2009 Financial Statements. GAO-11-174. Washington, D.C.: November 15, 2010.

Troubled Asset Relief Program: Opportunities Exist to Apply Lessons Learned from the Capital Purchase Program to Similarly Designed Programs and to Improve the Repayment Process. GAO-11-47. Washington, D.C.: October 4, 2010.

Troubled Asset Relief Program: Bank Stress Test Offers Lessons as Regulators Take Further Actions to Strengthen Supervisory Oversight. GAO-10-861. Washington, D.C.: September 29, 2010.

Financial Assistance: Ongoing Challenges and Guiding Principles Related to Government Assistance for Private Sector Companies. GAO-10-719. Washington, D.C.: August 3, 2010.

Troubled Asset Relief Program: Continued Attention Needed to Ensure the Transparency and Accountability of Ongoing Programs. GAO-10-933T. Washington, D.C.: July 21, 2010.

Management Report: Improvements are Needed in Internal Control Over Financial Reporting for the Troubled Asset Relief Program. GAO-10-743R. Washington, D.C.: June 30, 2010.

Troubled Asset Relief Program: Treasury's Framework for Deciding to Extend TARP Was Sufficient, but Could be Strengthened for Future Decisions. GAO-10-531. Washington, D.C.: June 30, 2010.

Troubled Asset Relief Program: Further Actions Needed to Fully and Equitably Implement Foreclosure Mitigation Programs. GAO-10-634. Washington, D.C.: June 24, 2010.

Debt Management: Treasury Was Able to Fund Economic Stabilization and Recovery Expenditures in a Short Period of Time, but Debt Management Challenges Remain. GAO-10-498. Washington, D.C.: May 18, 2010.

Troubled Asset Relief Program: Update of Government Assistance Provided to AIG. GAO-10-475. Washington, D.C.: April 27, 2010.

Troubled Asset Relief Program: Automaker Pension Funding and Multiple Federal Roles Pose Challenges for the Future. GAO-10-492. Washington, D.C.: April 6, 2010.

Troubled Asset Relief Program: Home Affordable Modification Program Continues to Face Implementation Challenges. GAO-10-556T. Washington, D.C.: March 25, 2010.

Troubled Asset Relief Program: Treasury Needs to Strengthen Its Decision-Making Process on the Term Asset-Backed Securities Loan Facility. GAO-10-25. Washington, D.C.: February 5, 2010.

Troubled Asset Relief Program: The U.S. Government Role as Shareholder in AIG, Citigroup, Chrysler, and General Motors and Preliminary Views on its Investment Management Activities. GAO-10-325T. Washington, D.C.: December 16, 2009.

Financial Audit: Office of Financial Stability (Troubled Asset Relief Program) Fiscal Year 2009 Financial Statements. GAO-10-301. Washington, D.C.: December 9, 2009.

Troubled Asset Relief Program: Continued Stewardship Needed as Treasury Develops Strategies for Monitoring and Divesting Financial Interests in Chrysler and GM. GAO-10-151. Washington, D.C.: November 2, 2009.

Troubled Asset Relief Program: One Year Later, Actions Are Needed to Address Remaining Transparency and Accountability Challenges. GAO-10-16. Washington, D.C.: October 8, 2009.

Troubled Asset Relief Program: Capital Purchase Program Transactions for October 28, 2008, through September 25, 2009, and Information on Financial Agency Agreements, Contracts, Blanket Purchase Agreements, and Interagency Agreements Awarded as of September 18, 2009. GAO-10-24SP. Washington, D.C.: October 8, 2009.

Debt Management: Treasury Inflation Protected Securities Should Play a Heightened Role in Addressing Debt Management Challenges. GAO-09-932. Washington, D.C.: September 29, 2009.

Troubled Asset Relief Program: Status of Efforts to Address Transparency and Accountability Issues. GAO-09-1048T. Washington, D.C.: September 24, 2009.

Troubled Asset Relief Program: Status of Government Assistance Provided to AIG. GAO-09-975. Washington, D.C.: September 21, 2009.

Troubled Asset Relief Program: Treasury Actions Needed to Make the Home Affordable Modification Program More Transparent and Accountable. GAO-09-837. Washington, D.C.: July 23, 2009.

Troubled Asset Relief Program: Status of Efforts to Address Transparency and Accountability Issues. GAO-09-920T. Washington, D.C.: July 22, 2009.

Troubled Asset Relief Program: Status of Participants' Dividend Payments and Repurchases of Preferred Stock and Warrants. GAO-09-889T. Washington, D.C.: July 9, 2009.

Troubled Asset Relief Program: June 2009 Status of Efforts to Address Transparency and Accountability Issues. GAO-09-658. Washington, D.C.: June 17, 2009.

Troubled Asset Relief Program: Capital Purchase Program Transactions for October 28, 2008, through May 29, 2009, and Information on Financial Agency Agreements, Contracts, Blanket Purchase Agreements, and Interagency Agreements Awarded as of June 1, 2009. GAO-09-707SP. Washington, D.C.: June 17, 2009.

Auto Industry: Summary of Government Efforts and Automakers' Restructuring to Date. GAO-09-553. Washington, D.C.: April 23, 2009.

Troubled Asset Relief Program: March 2009 Status of Efforts to Address Transparency and Accountability Issues. GAO-09-504. Washington, D.C.: March 31, 2009.

Troubled Asset Relief Program: Capital Purchase Program Transactions for the Period October 28, 2008 through March 20, 2009 and Information on Financial Agency Agreements, Contracts, and Blanket Purchase Agreements Awarded as of March 13, 2009. GAO-09-522SP. Washington, D.C.: March 31, 2009.

Troubled Asset Relief Program: March 2009 Status of Efforts to Address Transparency and Accountability Issues. GAO-09-539T. Washington, D.C.: March 31, 2009.

Troubled Asset Relief Program: Status of Efforts to Address Transparency and Accountability Issues. GAO-09-484T. Washington, D.C.: March 19, 2009.

Federal Financial Assistance: Preliminary Observations on Assistance Provided to AIG. GAO-09-490T. Washington, D.C.: March 18, 2009.

Troubled Asset Relief Program: Status of Efforts to Address Transparency and Accountability Issues. GAO-09-474T. Washington, D.C.: March 11, 2009.

Troubled Asset Relief Program: Status of Efforts to Address Transparency and Accountability Issues. GAO-09-417T. Washington, D.C.: February 24, 2009.

Troubled Asset Relief Program: Status of Efforts to Address Transparency and Accountability Issues. GAO-09-359T. Washington, D.C.: February 5, 2009.

Troubled Asset Relief Program: Status of Efforts to Address Transparency and Accountability Issues. GAO-09-296. Washington, D.C.: January 30, 2009.

Troubled Asset Relief Program: Additional Actions Needed to Better Ensure Integrity, Accountability, and Transparency. GAO-09-266T. Washington, D.C.: December 10, 2008.

Auto Industry: A Framework for Considering Federal Financial Assistance. GAO-09-247T. Washington, D.C.: December 5, 2008.

Auto Industry: A Framework for Considering Federal Financial Assistance. GAO-09-242T. Washington, D.C.: December 4, 2008.

Troubled Asset Relief Program: Status of Efforts to Address Defaults and Foreclosures on Home Mortgages. GAO-09-231T. Washington, D.C.: December 4, 2008.

Troubled Asset Relief Program: Additional Actions Needed to Better Ensure Integrity, Accountability, and Transparency. GAO-09-161. Washington, D.C.: December 2, 2008.

GAO's Mission	The Government Accountability Office, the audit, evaluation, and investigative arm of Congress, exists to support Congress in meeting its constitutional responsibilities and to help improve the performance and accountability of the federal government for the American people. GAO examines the use of public funds; evaluates federal programs and policies; and provides analyses, recommendations, and other assistance to help Congress make informed oversight, policy, and funding decisions. GAO's commitment to good government is reflected in its core values of accountability, integrity, and reliability.
Obtaining Copies of GAO Reports and Testimony	The fastest and easiest way to obtain copies of GAO documents at no cost is through GAO's website (www.gao.gov). Each weekday afternoon, GAO posts on its website newly released reports, testimony, and correspondence. To have GAO e-mail you a list of newly posted products, go to www.gao.gov and select "E-mail Updates."
Order by Phone	The price of each GAO publication reflects GAO's actual cost of production and distribution and depends on the number of pages in the publication and whether the publication is printed in color or black and white. Pricing and ordering information is posted on GAO's website, http://www.gao.gov/ordering.htm. Place orders by calling (202) 512-6000, toll free (866) 801-7077, or TDD (202) 512-2537. Orders may be paid for using American Express, Discover Card, MasterCard, Visa, check, or money order. Call for additional information.
Connect with GAO	Connect with GAO on Facebook, Flickr, Twitter, and YouTube. Subscribe to our RSS Feeds or E-mail Updates. Listen to our Podcasts. Visit GAO on the web at www.gao.gov.
To Report Fraud, Waste, and Abuse in Federal Programs	Contact: Website: www.gao.gov/fraudnet/fraudnet.htm E-mail: fraudnet@gao.gov Automated answering system: (800) 424-5454 or (202) 512-7470
Congressional Relations	Katherine Siggerud, Managing Director, SiggerudK@gao.gov, (202) 512-4400, U.S. Government Accountability Office, 441 G Street NW, Room 7125, Washington, DC 20548
Public Affairs	Chuck Young, Managing Director, youngc1@gao.gov, (202) 512-4800 U.S. Government Accountability Office, 441 G Street NW, Room 7149 Washington, DC 20548

Please Print on Recycled Paper.